EXPLORE THE WORLD

CH00919705

MALLORCA

Author:
Sebastian Melmoth

An Up-to-date travel guide
with 38 color photos
and 9 maps

NELLES

LEGEND / IMPRINT

Dear Reader,

Being up-to-date is the main goal of the Nelles series. Our correspondents help keep us abreast of the latest developments in the travel scene, while our cartographers see to it that the maps are kept completely current. However, as the travel world is constantly changing, we cannot guarantee that all of the information contained in our books is always valid. Should you come across a discrepancy, please contact us at: Nelles Verlag, Schleissheimer Str. 371B, D-80935 Munich, Germany, tel: +(49) 89 35 71 940, fax: +(49) 89 35 71 94 30, e-mail: Nelles.Verlag@t-online.de.

Note: Distances and measurements, including temperatures, used in this guide are metric. For conversion information, please see the *Guidelines* section of this book.

LEGEND

★★	Main Attraction *(on map)*	Escorca *(Town)* Places Highlighted
★★	*(in text)*	Sa Calobra *(Sight)* in Yellow Appear in Text
★	Worth Seeing *(on map)*	International airport
★	*(in text)*	
❽	Orientation Number in Text and on Map	**Alfabia** 1067 Mountain peak (altitude in meters)
▪	Public or Significant Building	\ 13 / Distance in kilometers
■	Hotel	Beach
▨	Market	Road closed to motor vehicles
🛈	Touristinformation	Tower, Lighthouse
✝ ⛪	Church	Ancient site, Cave
⛪ ⛫	Monastery, Castle	Fortress, Golf Course

▬▬▬	Expressway
══	Throughway
▬▬	Principal Highway
──	Main Road
──	Provincial Road
──	Secondary Road
----	Path
⟶	Ferry
⊜⊜⊜	Luxury Hotel Category
⊜⊜	Moderate Hotel Category
⊜	Budget Hotel Category *(for price information see "Accomodation" in Guidelines section)*

MALLORCA
© Nelles Verlag GmbH, 80935 München
   All rights reserved

First Edition 2001
ISBN 3-88618-715-2 (Nelles Travel Pack)
ISBN 3-88618-734-9 (Nelles Pocket)
Printed in Slovenia

Publisher:	Günter Nelles	**Translation:**	Janet Mayer
Managing Editor:	Berthold Schwarz	**Printed by:**	Gorenjski Tisk
Photo Editor:	K. Bärmann-Thümmel	**Lithos:**	Priegnitz, Munich
English Edition Editor:	Rebekah Rollo	**Cartography:**	Nelles Verlag GmbH

TABLE OF CONTENTS

LIST OF MAPS

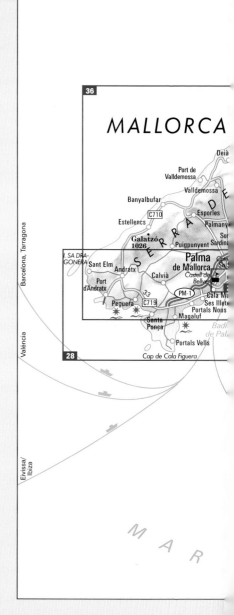

Note: Catalan place names have been used in the maps and in the text, even though the Spanish version of many names is still used.

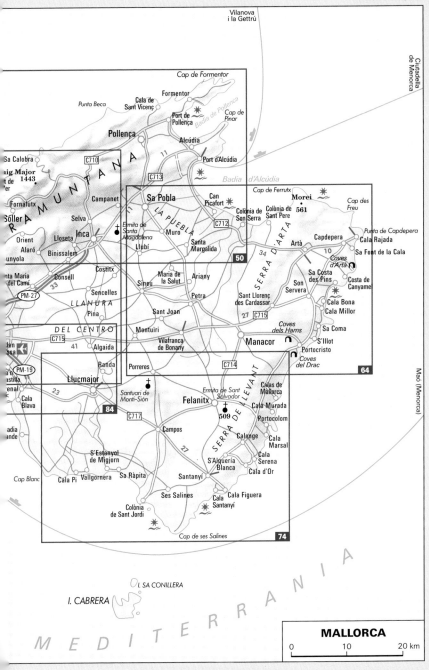

EARLY HISTORY

5th Century B.C. Neolithic finds in the grottos of Son Muleta and Son Matge are the earliest evidence of settlements on Mallorca.

2nd Century B.C. *Navetes*, *Taules* and *Talayots*, settlements and burial places carved out of chalk, are proof of migration from the eastern Mediterranean (*Talayot culture*).

PUNIC RULE

7th-3rd Century B.C. The Carthaginians found colonies on the Balearic Islands of Ibiza and Menorca; Mallorca also comes under Punic influence.

264-241 B.C. In the First Punic War the Mallorcans fight with Carthage against Rome

219-201 B.C. In the Second Punic War Carthage loses the Balearic Islands. Until the islanders are absorbed into the Roman Empire, they make a living from piracy.

ROMAN RULE

123/122 B.C. The Romans conquer the Balearic Islands. They found the Mallorcan cities of Palma, Capdepera, Manacor and Alaró; Pollentia becomes the capital. The centuries that follow are mostly peaceful. Olive and wine cultivation, introduced by the Romans, as well as ceramic craftsmanship, lead to prosperity.

3rd Century A.D. Christianity expands on Mallorca. Many Roman temples are turned into churches.

VANDAL RULE

A.D. 465 The Balearic Islands are conquered by the Vandal ruler Geiseric.

From ca. 500 persecution of Christians begins, under Geiseric's son, King Huneric. About 5000 Christians are deported from the islands to the Sahara.

EASTERN ROMAN-BYZANTINE RULE

534 Under Emperor Justinian, the Balearic Islands fall to the Byzantines, however, Constantinople's influence remains moderate.

Mid-7th Century Christianity is strengthened on the Balearic Islands by North African immigrants who are seeking refuge from new Moslem rulers.

From 707 pirate ships sail from the Moroccan coast to attack Mallorca. Raids by Mallorcan pirates also increase.

MOORISH RULE

902 The Moors take over the islands and stay for the next 300 years. Pollentia, which was destroyed by the Vandals, is rebuilt and renamed Alcúdia. The cultivated terraces at Estellencs and Banyalbufar are reminders of the Arabian knowledge of irrigation, as are the wind-powered water pumps in the lowlands around Palma and Sa Pobla. The Gardens of Alfabia are a testimony of the culture of the Saracens, under whose rule the island experienced a golden age.

Moorish warriors await James I of Aragón and his fleet in the Bay of Santa Ponça (fresco, ca. 1280).

1203 The Balearic Islands are ruled by the Almohad dynasty and the Christian faith is suppressed.

ARAGONESE MALLORCA

1229 As part of the *Reconquista*, King James I of Aragón reconquers Mallorca for Christianity.

1230 The foundation stone for Palma's cathedral is laid.

1276 James II founds the Kingdom of Mallorca.

1349 James III falls in the Battle of Llucmayor while fighting the Aragonese. As a result, the Balearic Islands are returned to the Kingdom of Aragón.

SPANISH MALLORCA

From 1479 the new Spanish dynasty of Aragón-Castilla has little interest in the Balearic Islands. The discovery of North America results in trade being centered in the Andalusian ports. The Inquisition and the expulsion of the Jews cause new crises in Mallorca. The upper-middle classes try to find other

Almond trees, along with peach plantations and citrus groves, have characterized the island's landscape since the time of the Moors.

sources of income by purchasing new land, thus making many peasant farmers dependent on them; the peasants rebel.

1571 Pirate raids temporarily diminish after the victory of Spain over the Algerian-Turkish fleet in the Battle of Lepanto. This period of recovery brings new prosperity to Mallorca, which also benefits from the arrival of precious metals from the new colonies. The art of Mallorca's gold- and silversmiths attains a

high standard, as demonstrated by splendid church altars found on the island, even in small villages.

1701-13 In the War of the Spanish Succession, the Mallorcan people side with the Hapsburgs under Archduke Charles II of Austria after he invades their island. The nobility, who sympathize with the Bourbon rulers, are expelled. In the Treaty of Utrecht (1713), however, Mallorca is awarded to Philip V of the House of Bourbon and thus remains Spanish.

1830 Piracy in the Mediterranean comes to an end.

1838 The beginning of the reign of Isabella II of Spain sees the secularization of all monasteries.

1890 A mildew epidemic destroys all the island's vineyards. Only after new, resistant varieties from California are introduced is wine production revived.

1895 Loss of the Spanish colonies results in an economic crisis on Mallorca. Many people emigrate to South America and Algeria.

1902 The city wall of Palma has to be demolished; one quarter of all 250,000 Mallorcans live in the capital.

1935 50,000 overnight guests are recorded. The first hotels are built in Can Pastilla and Cala d'Or.

1936-1939 During the Spanish Civil War there are battles between Franco's troops and the Republicans near Porto Cristo, with heavy losses. During World War II, Mallorca escapes greater suffering, thanks to Spain's neutral position.

1939-1975 During the Franco dictatorship all cultural independence is suppressed and islanders are forbidden to speak their own language, *Mallorcan*.

1950 Mass tourism begins.

1973 The *Grup Balear d'Ornitologia i Defensa de la Naturalesa* (GOB) is founded. The association has successfully fought for the creation of nature preserves on Mallorca.

1975 Under King Juan Carlos I, the increased regionalization and democratization of Spain enable Mallorca to gradually regain the independence it lost in 1349.

1983 The Spanish archipelago becomes autonomous.

Since 1990 six million tourists annually ensure Mallorcans the highest per capita income in Spain. The government attempts to prevent the negative effects of this onslaught (construction boom, destruction of nature) and to shake off the island's image as a land of cheap tourism.

PALMA DE MALLORCA

OLD TOWN
AROUND PALMA'S HARBOR
POBLE ESPANYOL
CASTELL DE BELLVER
MIRÓ MUSEUM

★★PALMA DE MALLORCA

History

The city of **★★Palma** was founded by the Romans in 123 B.C., after they sent a fleet of ships to subdue the audacious Mallorcan pirates. (Today its population is 320,000.) The Romans immediately began a sweeping program of "Romanization"; they established new towns, constructed roads and introduced new crops. The town of *Palmneria* (Palm of Victory) on the southwestern coast was administrated by Roman veterans and colonists and soon became a thriving metropolis.

In A.D. 902, Mallorca (also spelled Majorca) fell to the Moors, but Palma maintained its preeminent position. The Moslems, who made it their capital, renamed it *Medina Mayurka*. They also enlarged the city and enhanced it with their magnificent architecture. The Almudaina Palace was the seat of government and next to it a huge mosque towered above the city's narrow streets. For 300 years there was peace and prosperity.

Previous Pages: A narrow street in picturesque Fornalutx. A terrace restaurant in Port d'Andratx, one of Mallorca's prettiest marinas. Left: Taking a cigarette break on the elegant Avinguda Jaume III.

During the *Reconquista*, the Christian King James I (Catalan: *Jaume I*) conquered the city in 1229, and opened it to plunderers. Many valuable cultural objects disappeared as the booty of marauding bands of soldiers. Everything else was set on fire.

After centuries of peace and economic growth, due above all to its maritime trade, Palma was once again plundered in 1521; This time because of an insurrection by small peasant farmers.

Its free maritime trade came to an abrupt end with the victory of the Turkish pirates, the Barbarossa brothers, over the Spanish. The island population now suffered under the repeated attacks of the corsairs. The city of Palma itself escaped damage, but productive sea trade came to an almost complete standstill. It wasn't until after the Battle of Lepanto that the terror of the Ottoman piracy was finally brought to an end.

Palma also experienced great hardship during the Spanish Civil War, from 1936 to 1939. Not just the capital city, but the entire island suffered under the bombing attacks of fascist troops. However, during World War II things remained peaceful, largely because of Spain's neutral position.

In the middle of the 1950s, the growing tourist industry began to leave its traces on the island, above all in Palma. The city expanded beyond the city limits and, in an unparalleled construction boom, hotels and apartment houses were built practically overnight. Fortunately the historical old town center remained largely unaffected by the wide-spread construction offences that were committed in these years.

It wasn't until the early 1970s that Palma confronted the destructive results of unregulated mass tourism. This realization is the reason that, in Mallorca's metropolis, a considerable number of old, run-down hotels from the beginning of the construction frenzy were demolished, and parks and gardens were laid out in their place.

★★THE OLD TOWN

The actual, historical **★★Old Town**, known as **La Portella**, extends around the cathedral, the Almudaina Palace and the Episcopal Palace, and dates back to the Moorish settlement. Although hardly anything remains from that period, at least the narrow crooked alleyways, the shady little streets and the tiny squares are a reminder of the labyrinthine construction style of oriental *medinas* (cities).

The spacious **Parc de la Mar** ❶, directly below the imposing cathedral, is the classic starting point for a sightseeing tour of the old town. On the wall facing the coast road there is a huge **mural by Juan Miró**. Spread throughout the whole park area is an exhibition of modern sculptures by young artists.

The **Llull Monument** ❷, located on a traffic island that is covered with greenery, which seems to defy the onslaught of cars along the busy coast road, is also worth a look. Saint Raimundus Llull, or Ramón, who worked as a missionary in Algeria, is considered to be one of the island's most important philosophers.

From the monument, the wide Avinguda d'Antonio Maura leads towards the

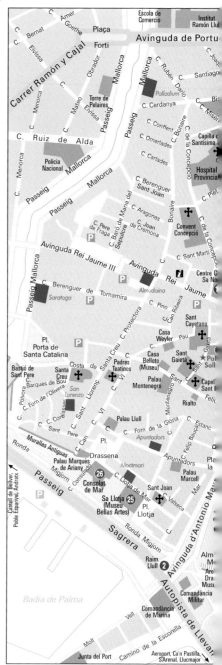

PALMA DE MALLORCA / OLD TOWN

Palma de Mallorca

PALMA'S OLD TOWN

0   100   200 m

15

old town center. In the shady green spaces on the right hand side of the street, directly below the impressive façade of the palace, the ladies of the royal court once amused themselves in the **King's Gardens** ❸ (*S'Hort del Rei*). Today, even amidst the noise of the city, you can still find a peaceful oasis between shade trees, glorious flowers from southern latitudes and playfully designed fountains.

In the gardens, a wide arch spans a small pond. Beside the pond are casemates (*Ses Voltes*), the oldest parts of which are of Roman and Moorish origin. These defensive constructions were restored in the early 1990s and since then, up-and-coming artists have been given the opportunity to exhibit their work here.

Several flights of stairs lead up to the **viewing terrace** on the south side of the cathedral. From here you have an excellent view of the bay and Palma's harbor.

Above: In the King's Gardens. Right: Palma at night – Catedral Sa Seu and the Almudaina Palace.

The *Almudaina Palace ❹ (*Palau de l'Almudaina*) was the residence of the emir during the rule of the Moors. After extensive alterations, which were carried out by Mallorcan and Aragonese kings, almost nothing remains of the original structure. Only a few of the royal chambers are open for to the public, including the Santa Ana chapel, in Gothic style with an older Romanesque portal, and the small church of *del Pellaires*, in the flamboyant style of the late French Gothic Period.

**Cathedral of Sa Seu

The **Cathedral ❺ *(Catedral Sa Seu)* is one of the Balearic Islands' most important art historical sights. During the Moorish period this elevated site was the location of the main mosque of the Islamic city *Medina Mayurka*. Immediately after he had conquered the city, King James I ordered the construction of a church for Christian worship. In order to make room for this ambitious undertaking, the surrounding buildings and part of the large mosque were torn down. In 1269, the apse, which faces east, was completed and dedicated. In 1338, large sections of the side aisles were also finished.

Despite the collapse of the ceiling in 1490, by 1587 the cathedral was finally nearing completion, and it was then given the required godly blessing. The final exterior, which is an execution of plans by the gifted architect Antoni Guadí, wasn't completed until the beginning of the 20th century.

The cathedral's **main portal**, which is directly opposite the Almudaina Palace, is only opened on especially festive occasions. After an earthquake in 1851 caused severe damage in the area near the portal, the entire façade was completely redone. The portal is in the plateresque style, with rich detail, and is fashioned on a triumphal arch. It stands out in sharp contrast to

the majestic, but less lavishly decorated form of the rest of the building.

The tourist entrance to the cathedral is on the north side, facing away from the sea, through what was once the poor house. From here you can enter the substructure of the 48-meter-high bell tower. This is where you will find the **Vermell Sacristy**, which today forms part of the cathedral museum.

In the center of the neighboring **Gothic Chapter Room**, you can see the tomb of Bishop Gil Sanchez Muñoz, who was intended to succeed the Antipope Benedict XIII in Avignon, but who stepped down in favor of the Pope in Rome; in recognition of this fact he was ordained the Bishop of Mallorca. In the adjacent **New Chapter Room**, which was constructed in the Gothic style during the 17th century, there are ecclesiastical treasures of almost inestimable value on display. The Gothic monstrance of gold-plated silver is 2.28 meters high and weighs 120 kilograms. It is adorned with 230 pearls and 826 diamonds. Of even greater value, and

of even greater spiritual worth, are the relics that are preserved in this room. A **wooden cross** (*Relicuario de la Vera Cruz*), set in gold and decorated with an abundance of jewels, is supposed to be the largest reliquary of Christendom. Yet another golden reliquary (*Relicuario de las Santas Espinas*) – relic of the holy thorns – is shaped like a Gothic church with three towers. The three thorns in the middle of the building are supposed to be from the crown of thorns of the Redeemer. In other reliquaries there are allegedly pieces of the scourge with which Jesus was whipped, remains of the robe of the Redeemer, and pieces of the sponge with which he was offered vinegar and water to drink. One of the more conspicuous exhibits is a forearm made of silver and said to contain remnants of the bones of Saint Sebastian, the patron saint of the inhabitants of Palma.

From the old Gothic chapter room you can enter the cathedral, which is distinguished from all other Gothic churches in Europe by its huge dimensions, its unusually slender columns and its unique rose windows. The cathedral covers an area of 6600 square meters and measures 109 meters in length, i.e., longer than a football field! It is one-third wider than the cathedral in Milan, and three times as wide as the cathedral in Cologne. Furthermore, its octagonal columns, despite reaching twice as high as those in Cologne, are one-third more slender.

The largest of the seven magnificent **rose windows** is placed above the high altar. With a diameter of 12.5 meters, this is the largest Gothic rose window in the world. There are no fewer than 1236 red, yellow and blue panes, arranged in a geometric, arabesque pattern that covers an impressive area of 123 square meters.

The canopy-like construction above the simple, marble main alter, is an addition from the 20th century, and is based on a design by the Catalan architect Antoni Gaudí. It depicts an oversized crown symbolizing the royal dignity of the Redeemer. The 35 lanterns that are suspended from it and the transparent stones, which are illuminated from the inside, create very special lighting effects.

The cathedral contains a total of 19 chapels, which are distributed along the side aisles, the choir and the (north-) west façade. These are dedicated to the Savior, the Mother of God and saints of the Roman Catholic Church, and date from several different centuries.

The furnishings of the ****Corpus Christi Chapel** (*Capella de Corpus Cristi*) are particularly interesting. It has a baroque altar, carved by Jaume Blanquer, and is considered one of the most significant works of art of its time. The high relief, directly above the altar table, shows Jesus and the disciples at the Last Supper, and is impressive not only because of its unusual diagonal perspective, but even more for the strong expression of the fig-

Right: The Arabian Baths – a reminder of the Moorish lifestyle.

ures. In the shell-shaped niches beside the plateresque double columns, there are figures of Saint Matthew and Saint John. Above this, you can see Saint Francis of Assisi and Saint Francis of Paula, the Holy Family in the Temple, and right at the top there is a depiction of the Temptations of Saint Anthony.

Continuing the Walking Tour Of the Old Town

The tourist exit from the cathedral is on the east side, and a sign reading *Museu Diocesà* leads you to the viewing terrace. Take a minute to stop and take a few steps back in order to get a view of the cathedral's glorious ****south portal** from the outside. It is one of the most important masterpieces of Spanish Gothic work. The wonderful decoration, with realistic figures, is largely the work of Guillermo Sagrera, the Mallorcan sculptor who, in recognition of his work here, was also commissioned to design the building for the Maritime Stock Exchange.

The **Diocesan Museum** ❻ (*Museu Diocesà*) is housed in the part of the Episcopal Palace that is directly next to the cathedral's south portal. It displays, in addition to some rather insignificant curiosities from around the world, finds from the Talayot and Roman periods, Arabian ceramics, Gothic altar pieces, and valuable 15ht-century paintings and books.

The ***Museum of Mallorca** ❼ (*Museu de Mallorca*) is located in a wonderful palace that was built for Count Ayamans in 1634. The exhibition, which is clearly structured, communicates a complete picture of the island's history from prehistoric times until the 19th century. The exhibits range from the early Talayot culture through the Roman period, up to the Arabian settlement. Stonemasonry, ceramics, craft work in the Mudejar style, and numerous paintings and sculptures dating from the Middle Ages to the 19th century enhance the large collection.

The **Arabian Baths** ❽ (*Banys Arabs*), a small and inconspicuous bath house, are one of the last witnesses of the Moorish period. It dates from the 10th century and has two vaulted domes that are supported by fragile-looking columns.

From Carrer Puresa, you can walk along the narrow Carrer del Vent, to the church **Monte Sión** ❾ (*Església Monti-Sión*), which was built between 1571 and 1683, on the foundations of a demolished synagogue.

The ***Monastery of Sant Francesc** ❿ (San Francisco) is Mallorca's second-most important religious building, after the cathedral. The marvelous façade, with a beautiful rose window, depicting Saint George as he kills the dragon, and the baroque-plateresque portal with the Mother of God surrounded by angels, are the masterpieces of Francisco Herrera.

You enter the monastery's church and cloister through the building on the right, which is the monastery's school. The Gothic cloister with pointed arches, through which sunlight can flood the courtyard, the delicate colonnade and the carefully maintained garden form a composition of perfect harmony. The interior of the church can seem, in contrast, to be rather dark, at least when you first go inside.

In the fifth side chapel on the left-hand-side, is the final resting place of Ramón Llull, a saint and one of Europe's the most important clergymen.

The **Church of Santa Eulalia** ⓫ was originally built by James I during the *Reconquest*. It was altered many times in the following centuries, which has led to an interesting mixture of styles, including Gothic, baroque and Renaissance. Mallorca's most famous painter, Guillermo Mezquida (1625-1747), decorated the main altar with a beautiful and expressive painting of the Coronation of Mary.

Follow Carrer Morey, the street opposite the church portal, turning right at the next corner. You will arrive at the **Almudaina Arch** ⓬ (*Arc de l'Almudaina*), which was once part of the city gate to the old Moslem capital *Medina Mayurka*.

From the next corner it is only a few steps to the right to the lively **Plaça Cort**, (the city hall square) in the center of the old town.

The **City Hall** 🔞 (*Ajuntament*) is hard to miss because it stands, covered with flags, between other buildings that are typical of the same period. This 17th-century building successfully unites elements of both the Spanish baroque and the Italian Renaissance styles. Pay special attention to the carved wooden caryatides that support the overhanging roof.

The **Plaça Major** 🔞, a large rectangular square in the heart of the city, is bordered an all four sides by attractive houses with arcades. There are many street cafés, ice cream parlors and restaurants that invite you to spend some time there, and a variety of street musicians who provide pleasant background music. Underground, there is a complete shopping center with many small shops that mostly cater to the needs of tourists.

The pedestrian zone **Carrer de Sant Miquel** leads to the north and is lined with shops for those with more exclusive tastes. The **Bank March** building (No. 11) houses the paintings and exhibits of the **★Fundació March** 🔞 (March Foundation), which includes works by Dalí, Picasso and March. The collection was that of Joan March, the island's shady billionaire.

Colorful fruit and fish stands are characteristic of the **market halls** 🔞 (*Mercat de l'Olivar*). Even those visitors who are not self-caterers and are not obliged to make purchases will find something of interest, e.g., delicious snacks from one of the many tapas bars.

Leave the market halls through the back entrance, and by keeping to the left you then come to a large square with green spaces – the **Plaça Espanya** 🔞. The bus station, the station for the "Red Lightning" train to Sóller, the train station for the line to Inca, and the municipal

Above: Shopping in the market halls (Mercat de l'Olivar). Right: The Gran Hotel, a beautiful art nouveau building, is now a museum.

tourist information office are located here. In the center of the busy square is an **equestrian statue of James I**. This is where the city gate stood during the Moorish period and where James' victorious *Reconquista* troops forced their way into the city on December 31, 1229.

If you head in the direction in which the bronze king is looking, you can walk along the Carrer dels Oms, a street that is closed to traffic and is lined with shops. A little further on, you come to the **Rambla**, a pleasant, wide avenue for walking, with a wide median strip on which kiosks selling flowers are lined up one after another.

The **Bank Sa Nostra** ⓲, located on a picturesque triangular plaza, regularly exhibits the works of young artists in its art gallery. Art lovers should not miss the opportunity to visit because it presents a rare opportunity to learn about contemporary Mallorcan painting.

The street leads downhill towards the busy avenue **Avinguda Jaume III**, a popular shopping street with airy arcades that protect from both sun and rain. Turn left and cross the square (Plaça Rei Joan Carles I), which is lined with several inviting street cafés, then turn into the Carrer de la Unió – and a few steps further and you will be on the **Plaça Mercat**, a square that is surrounded by several impressive buildings.

The ★**Gran Hotel** ⓳ was built at the beginning of the 20th century and is a beautiful example of the art nouveau style. It was, inside and out, a very attractive luxury hotel and a place where the wealthy of the world found an elegant place to stay. Today it houses a **museum** for Mallorcan art from the 19th and 20th centuries, a café and a bookshop.

The **Can Berga Palace** ⓴ was built on Moorish foundations shortly after the *Reconquista*. It was originally used as a convent, but 400 years later it passed into the hands of the Berga family, who extensively remodeled and added to. Today, it houses Mallorca's judicial authority.

Next to the palace you will see the wonderful art nouveau façades of the ★**Can Casassayas** ㉑, which clearly show that they were inspired by the work of the great architect Antoni Gaudí.

The ★**Solleric Palace** ㉒ (*Palau Solleric*) is also worth seeing. It has a beautiful balcony with slender columns on the second floor of the front and its marvelous inner courtyard is definitely worth a short visit. The building recently underwent extensive renovations and is now *the* exhibition hall in Palma. A pretty café and a bookshop complete this impressive facility.

As you head towards the sea, it is worth taking a few steps to the right into the next side street (Sant Feliu). There you will find several especially attractive palaces that once belonged to Mallorca's noble families.

Like the city hall, the **Parliament Building** ㉓ (*Parlament Balear*), which is built in the neo-classical style, is also decorated with flags. In earlier times was a meeting place for Mallorca's social upper

Palma de Mallorca

strata, but in 1982 the building was purchased for use by the government of the Balearic Islands.

The **★March Palace** ㉔ (*Palau March*) was originally built for the island's billionaire, Joan March, in 1945. However, even with his extravagant city villa, the unscrupulous profiteer and nouveau-riche upstart never did manage to gain acceptance with the local upper classes who despised him and always thought of him as a shady character.

The church-like building known as **Sa Llotja** ㉕ was once the seat of Palma's Maritime Stock Exchange, which was of great importance throughout the whole Mediterranean. An angel with curly hair is resplendent above the portal and octagonal towers reach upward from the roof, are connected with each other by a crenellated wall into which small decorative towers are integrated. If you look through

Above: The artist Joan Miró, in 1967, working in his studio, which today forms part of the Miró Museum.

the leaded windows with their pointed arches, you will see columns that are formed with a spiral pattern supporting the vaulted ceiling. The building is now only used for special exhibitions.

The **Consolat de Mar** ㉖, a splendid building next to the former Maritime Stock Exchange, was built for the world-famous Mallorcan School of Seafaring during the 17th century. Unfortunately, soon after it was completed, a new court that was responsible for maritime trade was founded. Today, the building serves as the official seat of the Minister of the Balearic Islands regional government.

AROUND PALMA'S ★HARBOR

Heading away from **Parc de la Mar**, along the coast, you first reach the commercial harbor and then a much smaller breakwater with a **fishing harbor** ㉗ (*Moll Vell*) and the Royal Sailing Club (*Real Club Náutico*). Early risers won't want to miss the fish auction that is held in the nearby fish market.

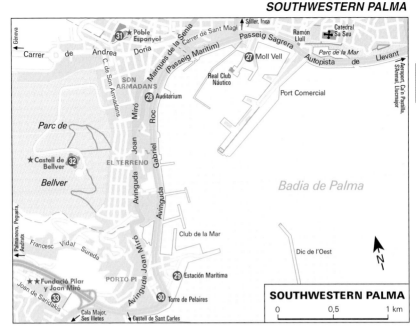

Next, after strolling past luxury yachts and motorboats, you will come first to the **Auditorium** ㉘, Palma's ultra-modern concert hall, and then the grounds of the *Club de la Mar* where the largest sailing and motor yachts are anchored.

Opposite is the **ferry port** ㉙ *(Estación Marítima)* for trips to Genoa, Barcelona, Alicante, Valencia and Marseilles.

Next you come to the oldest part of the harbor and the **Torre de Pelaires** ㉚, which was used, after the 15th century, as a quarantine ward. If you continue around the harbor basin you come to of the harbor area's former military zone. A reminder of this is the **Castell de Sant Carles**, a fortress from which the harbor could be watched and which now serves as the home to an interesting **Military Museum**.

POBLE ESPANYOL

Whoever likes to watch craftsmen at work or is interested in (copies of) historical structures will really enjoy a visit to the **Poble Espanyol** ㉛ (Spanish Village). It is actually more like a small Spanish town than a village – a fantasy construction made of reproductions of Spain's famous towers, gates, courtyards, town halls and churches. Astonishingly, a large number of different styles have been successfully combined to create a harmonious, complete picture.

*CASTELL DE BELLVER

The *Bellver Castle ㉜, high above the town, has amazingly managed to defy historical redevelopments for many centuries. From its heights above the city, visitors can enjoy a fascinating view of Mallorca's metropolis.

Immediately after the conquest of the island, James I ordered the construction of a fort to permanently secure the region. However, the work took a long time and the fort was not finished until 1309, some 80 years later. It was used only for a short time thereafter, as a prison and place for executions.

If the fort has a picturesque appearance for today's visitor, the circular structure, with its thick defensive walls and projecting fortified towers, must nevertheless have been a rather intimidating sight for would-be attackers. The circular inner courtyard with two-storied arcades is an interesting architectural mix – with Romanesque arches in the lower story and Gothic arches in the upper one. Today the Castell de Bellver is used by both the **Historical Museum** and by the island's government as representative setting for official receptions and concerts.

THE **MIRÓ MUSEUM

Palma's splendid avenue of the arts leads westwards, just beyond the ferry port and there becomes a major highway. The first exit (Cala Major) takes you to the *Marivent*, the summer residence of the Spanish royal family, and to the **Miró Museum** ㉝. It is a little hard to find, but violet signs indicating the direction of the *Fondació Pilar y Joan Miró* mark the way.

In 1956, the painter Joan Miró (1893-1983) bought a house here, set on a hill, where he also had his studio. In 1981 he and his wife Pilar initiated a foundation, by donating the buildings and surrounding grounds to the city of Palma.

You can visit the large **studio**, which was designed by the Spanish architect Josep Lluis Sert, one of Miró's friends. It was the wish of the artist that his studio be left exactly as it was before his death.

In 1993, in honor of his 100th birthday, the Miró Museum was completed by the Spanish architect Rafael Moneo. It is also located in the grounds and houses about 100 of Miró's paintings, some of them unfinished, around 1000 drawings and other works on paper, as well as 1500 letters. The museum also includes a library and an auditorium in which a short film, *Miró, the Light of Mallorca*, is shown daily.

PALMA DE MALLORCA

O.I.T. Municipal, Sant Domingo 11, tel: 971 724 090, fax: 971 720 240; for information about the city of Palma. **O.I.T. Municipal**, Plaça Espanya, tel: 971 711 527; for information about the city of Palma. **O.I.T. Airport**, tel/fax: 971 789556. **O.I.T. de Mallorca**, Plaça de la Reina 2, tel: 971 712 216. fax: 971 720251; for information about the island of Mallorca, bus and train schedules, etc.

Airport Son San Joan, 10 km east of the city center in Can Pastilla, central tel: 971 789 000. **Train Stations** for the "Red Lightning" to Sóller and for trains to Inca are at Plaça Espanya 2, tel: 971 752 051 and 971 752 245. **Long-distance buses** also leave from here. **Ferries** leave for Menorca once a week, for Ibiza und Barcelona daily. Departures from the Estació Maritima, tel: 971 405 014 and 971 405 360.

Son Vida, C. Reina z. Urb. Son Vida, tel: 971 790 000, fax: 971 790 017; luxury hotel, a palace dating from the 13th century, in a suburb of Palma, in the middle of a golf course, approx. 5 km from the city center. **Valparaiso Palace**. C. Vidal Sureta 23, tel: 971 400 300, fax: 971 405 904; in the villa suburb of Bonanova, with a wonderful panoramic view of Palma, four golf courses nearby, approx. 3 km from the city center. **Palacio Ca Sa Galesa**, C. de Miramar 8, tel: 971 715 400, fax: 971 721 579; luxurious palace hotel in the center of the old town, near the cathedral, furnished with antiques and art of all kinds. **Arabella Golf Hotel**, C. de la Vinagrella, tel: 971 799 999, fax: 971 799 997; luxurious inn at the Son Vide golf course, with attractive country-style architecture, approx. 5 km from the city center. **Read's**, only a few km from Palma in the small town of Santa Maria del Camí, tel: 971 140 261, fax: 971 140 762; luxury hotel in an old mansion, surrounded by palms and olive trees, has an outstanding restaurant.

Nixe Palace, Av. Joan Miró 269, tel: 971 700 888, fax: 971 403 171; between Palma and Cala Major, was recently thoroughly renovated, over 100 rooms with sea views. **San Lorenzo**, C. San Lorenzo 14, tel: 971 728200, fax: 971 711 901; small hotel with just a few rooms in an old city palace, in the center of Palma. **Saratoga**, Passeig de Mallorca 6, tel: 971 727 240, fax: 971 727 312; half of the almost 200 rooms are reserved for business people, the other rooms are for tourists. **Hotel Born**, C. San Jaime 3, tel: 971 712 942, fax: 971 718 618; has the most imposing hotel foyer in all of Mallorca, a former city palace, in a quiet, central location. **Son Espases Nous**, Camino Son Espases 7, Secar de la Real, Agrotourisme-style (Rural Tourism) accommodation, reservations tel: 971 721-

508, fax: 971 717 317; approx. 5 km from city center, rooms in a mansion built in 1805, amidst fields that are still cultivated.

🌀 **Hostal Ritzi**, C. Apuntadores 6, tel/fax: 971 714 610; guesthouse in the city center, under English management. **Hostal Res. Terminus**, Eusebi Estada 2, tel: 971 750 014, fax: 971 204 139; guesthouse in an an art nouveau-style house, lots of atmosphere, situated near the Plaça Espanya.

❎ **Bon Lloc**. C. Sant Feliu 7, tel: 971 718 617; small vegetarian restaurant that offers good value for money, in a quiet street in the Llotja district. **Casa Eduardo**. Travessia Pesquera 4, tel: 971 711 182; directly on the fishing harbor, fish restaurant, has been very popular with Palma's locals for over 50 years. **Es Parlament**, C. del Conquistador 11, tel: 971 726 026; in the building of the Balearic Parliament, here the representatives of the governing assembly wine and dine, magnificent wall and ceiling decorations. **Koldo Royo**, Passeig Maritim 3, tel: 971 732 435; the Basque cook here has won several awards, the restaurant has one Michelin star. **Celler Sa Premsa**, Plaça Bisbe Berenguer de Palou 8, tel: 971 723 529; a basement restaurant/bar, popular with tourists, plain, hearty Mallorcan cuisine, in a Spanish folklore atmosphere: vaulted ceiling, old wine vats, simple wooden tables and chairs, with posters of bullfights dating from several decades on the walls. **Es Baluard**, Plaça Porta Santa Catalina 9, tel: 971 719 609; the best Mallorcan cuisine to be found anywhere. **Le Bistrot**, C. Teodor Llorente 6, tel: 971 287 175; simple, but good French bistro food. **Casa Fernando**, Ciutat de Jardin, Trafalgar 27, tel: 971 265 417; excellent fish restaurant. **Rififi**, C. Joan Miró 182, tel: 971 402 035; one of the best fish restaurants in Palma. **Caballito de Mar**, Passeig Sagrera 5, tel: 971 72 1074; the "little sea horse" is in the center of the Llotja district, very good fish dishes. **Samanthas**, Calle Francisco Vidal Sureda 115, tel: 971 700 000; an elegant restaurant in the suburb La Bonanova, international cuisine. **Marcelino**, C. Sant Llorenç 23, tel: 971 712 673; nothing extraordinary and rather simple, but very good fish restaurant, in the Llotja district. **La Lubina**, Muelle Viejo, tel: 971 723 350; good fish restaurant near the Parc de la Mar.

🍸 **Abacanto**, Camí de Son Nicolau; on the northern edge of the city in a handsome mansion, dating from the 18th century, with a large flower garden. The epitome of exclusiveness. **Tito's Palace**, Plaça Gomila 3; Palma's largest and best-known disco. **La Bóveda**, Boteria 3; tapas bar and "in" meeting place on the Plaça de la Llotja. **Can Joan de S'Aigo**, C. Sanc 10; old, established café that serves excellent cakes and pastries. This is where the painter Miró used to drink his hot chocolate. **Bar Bosch**, Plaça Rei Joan Carles I; in the eve-

nings the clientele is almost exclusively young. **Ábaco**. C. Sant Joan; one of the most popular bars of the island, located in a beautiful city palace. **La Red**, C. Concepció 5, tel: 971 713 574; internet-café.

🏛 **Almudaina Palace**, April-Sept: Mon-Fri 10 am-6:30 pm, Sat 10 am-2 pm, closed Sun; Oct-March: Mon-Fri 10 am-2 pm, 4-6 pm, Sat and Sun 10 am-2 pm. **Cathedral Sa Seu**, April-Sept: Mon-Fri 10 am-6 pm, Sat 10 am-2 pm, closed Sun; Oct-March: Mon-Fri 10 am-12:30 pm, 4-6:30 pm, Sat 10 am-2:30 pm, closed Sun. **Diocesan Museum**, April-Oct: daily 10 am-1:30 pm, 3-8 pm; Nov-March: Mon-Fri 10 am-1 pm, 3-6 pm, Sat and Sun 10 am-1 pm. **Museu de Mallorca**, Tue-Sat 10 am-2 pm, 4-7 pm, Sun 10 am-2 pm, closed Mon. **Banys Arabs** (Arabian Baths), April-Oct: daily 8:30 am-8 pm; Nov-March: daily 8:30 am-6 pm. **Convent de Sant Francesc**, Mon-Sat 9:30 am-12:30 pm, 3:30-6 pm, closed Sun. **Bank March**, Mon-Fri 10 am-6:30 pm, Sat 10 am-1:30 pm, closed Sun. **Castell de Sant Carles** (military museum), Mon-Sat 9 am-1 pm, 3-5 pm, closed Sun. **Castell de Bellver** (fortified castle), April-Sept: Mon-Sat 8 am-8 pm, closed Sun; Oct-March: Mon-Sat 8 am-6 pm, closed Sun. **Miró Museum**, Tue-Fri 10 am-7 pm, Sat 10 am-3 pm, closed Sun and Mon. **Poble Espanyol**, April-Nov: daily 9 am-8 pm; Dec-March: daily 9 am-6 pm.

➕ **Palma International Center for Medical Specialists** – **Porto Pi**, Porto Pi 8, 2nd floor, tel: 971 704 020, night tel: 971 707 035; specialists for urology, gynecology, ophthalmology, pediatrics, surgery, emergency medicine, ENT, allergies, internal medicine, cardiology and gastro-enterology. **Dentists**, Dr. Brandt, C. Olmos 7, tel: 971 717 553. Dr. Santha, C. Union 2a, tel: 971 718 873, emergencies: 929 689 068. **Hospital**, Son Dureta, C. Andrea Doria 55, tel: 971 175 000; state-run clinic with four interpreters. **Policlinica Miramar**, Vercinal La Vileta, tel: 971 450 212; private clinic.

🏪 **Market**, Mercat de l'Olivar, Plaça Olivar, Mon-Sat till 1 pm. **Flea Market**, El Rastro, Av. Gabriel Alomar Villalonga, Sat 8 am-1:30 pm. **Factory Outlet Center**, Center S.L., Av. Conde de Sallent 1, tel: 629 256 353; up to 50% off fashion brand names. **Forn des Teatre** (cake and pastry shop), Plaça Weyler; good bakery. The artistic decoration of the house's façade is a popular subject with photographers.

❎ **Main Post Office**, C. de la Constitució 5, tel: 971 721 867; Mon-Fri 8:30 am-8:30 pm, Sat 9:30 am-2 pm, closed Sun.

🎟 **Bullfighting Arena**: Plaça de Toros, bullfighing June-Sept: Sundays at 6 pm; also open-air concerts and TV events. **Sailing Regatta Copa del Rey**, annually, one week in August, information at Club Náutico (yacht club), tel: 971 726 848.

25

THE SOUTHWEST

RESORTS AROUND PALMA
PALMANOVA / MAGALUF
SANTA PONÇA
PEGUERA / CALA FORNELLS
PORT D'ANDRATX / ANDRATX
SANT ELM

The Southwest

RESORTS AROUND PALMA

Cala Major, Illetes and Gènova

If you avoid the PM-1, which runs southwest, and take the coast road C-719 instead, you soon reach **Cala Major ❶**, just beyond Palma's city limits. This tourist center, which has already expanded to Palma's city limits, is especially popular with Scandinavian and British visitors. The summer residence of the Spanish royal family, the *Palacio Marivent*, is located in Cala Major, as is the ****Miró Museum**, which is well worth visiting (for a detailed description see p. 24).

The nearby town of **Illetes ❷** is more inviting. Small, but goods hotels, summer homes and villas can be found here. This is an ideal destination for guests who wish to spend a beach or sporting vacation in a sophisticated environment near the island's capital city.

From here it is also not far to the **Coves de Gènova ❸**, which are admittedly not as spectacular as the large caves in the east of the island, but because of that fact, they are less overrun with visitors. The entrance to the stalactite cave, which can be explored with a half-hour-long guided

Left: As the shadows grow longer, the beach gets emptier.

tour, is located in the garden of the restaurant *Ses Coves*.

Bendinat and Portals Nous

North of **Bendinat** is the fort **Castell de Bendinat**, which was constructed by the Christian conqueror James I. The fortress was converted into a Neo-Gothic-style feudal palace during the 18th century. Unfortunately, it is no longer possible for the general public to visit the grounds.

Portals Nous ❹, a "planned community" from the 1930s, has grown enough to almost reach Bendinat's city limits. The royal sailing yacht *Fortuna* docks in its exclusive boating harbor **Port Portals**. Here, in Mallorca's most elegant marina, sailboats and motor yachts from all over the world lie side by side at anchor and the normal tourist can become giddy when he sees the dimensions of some of these ships. With a length of just over 20 meters, King Juan Carlos' yacht the *Fortuna* is in fact, in comparison to some of these floating palaces, rather small. The harbor promenade is lined with all kinds of bars, cafés and good restaurants. The beautiful and successful people especially like to dine on the terrace at *Esdi's* or to indulge themselves at *Tristan*, another excellent restaurant.

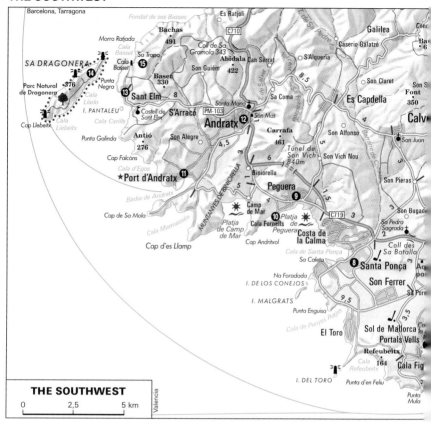

THE SOUTHWEST

0   2,5   5 km

An attraction on the southwestern edge of town is **Marineland**, an amusement park that is of special interest to children. Here, dolphins jump through hoops, sea lions show off their considerable skills, and multitudes of colorful parrots all try to scream louder than the others.

PALMANOVA AND MAGALUF

The towns of **Palmanova ❺** and **Magaluf ❻** are in complete contrast to the more country-like atmosphere of Portals Nous. These boomtowns of tourism, with their "hotel skylines," have quickly expanded to become one built-up area. Pubs and "fish & chip" shops cater to the taste of the many British vacationers.

These towns also offer a wide-ranging spectrum of entertainment. Laid out between artificial lakes and waterfalls, caves and tropical gardens, you will find **Golf Fantasia**, a large mini-golf course. From Magaluf, you can take a submarine trip to the depths of the Mediterranean Sea in the **Nemo**. You can play a few rounds of golf on the nearby golf course, or while away the time in Europe's largest disco, the **BCM**, or in Mallorca's only casino, the **Palladium**. In **Dorado City**, lovers of nightlife can find bars, discos and all kind of entertainment. If you prefer to be entertained during the day, you can visit the **Aquapark**, where pools, slides, Bravo – a 124-meter-long rafting river, bars, ice cream parlors and res-

this time from the mid-1950s. On the north side of town one hotel after another was quickly built. The south side was reserved for the construction of private villas and small vacation homes. To raise the overall standard of the resort, the promenade along the beach, which is small and generally very crowded, has been redesigned and planted with greenery.

In 1229, led by James I, the fleet of the Christian *Reconquista* armies sailed into the Bay of Santa Ponça and anchored off the Sa Caleta Peninsula. Just three and a half months later, the king had conquered Mallorca and thereafter he called himself *el Conqueridor*, the conqueror. Seven hundred years later, a memorial cross was set on a steep rocky spur. Eight relief panels at the plinth of the **Creu de la Conquesta** narrate the historical events. To get to the memorial cross, leave the center of Santa Ponça and follow the signs to *Club Náutico*. The cross is located above the marina restaurant on the tip of the Sa Caleta Peninsula.

PEGUERA AND CALA FORNELLS

Peguera ❾ is also purely a vacation resort, but it is dominated by German tourists. Despite all the tourists, since the town's main street has been almost completely closed to traffic and the beach was recently refilled with sand, the quality of life here has noticeably improved and the place has become much more attractive.

From Peguera, a small road leads uphill to **Cala Fornells ❿**, a very quiet villa resort with summer homes perched high up on the hill. From here, the view of the Santa Ponça Bay is excellent.

There is no mass-tourism here for the simple reason that available accommodation is limited and sun-seeking tourists would find it too far removed from the nearest sandy beach. Indeed, you have to walk downhill along a narrow road in order to get to the small beach, which is covered with stones.

taurants await a public of children and adults alike.

One rewarding excursion leads to the **Cova de la Mare Déu ❼**, a cave shrine at **Portals Vells**. According to tradition, a Genoese captain established the shrine out of gratitude for a miraculous deliverance from great danger at sea.

SANTA PONÇA

Santa Ponça ❽ is well known for its two golf courses, one of which is only open to members of the local club. Large golf championships, including the *Balearic Open*, are hosted on the second.

The town, situated on the cliffs above the bay, is another "planned community,"

*PORT D'ANDRATX AND ANDRATX

A route through an enchantingly beautiful landscape leads from Camp de Mar to ***Port d'Andratx ⓫**, one of Mallorca's most attractive harbor and yachting resorts. Along the harbor basin there is a pleasant promenade with many very fine restaurants, and it is refreshing to find that there are no souvenir kiosks or large hotel blocks. Some of the streets are closed to traffic and there is a large parking lot on the edge of town.

Five kilometers inland is **Andratx ⓬**. The fertile region between the harbor town and the small country town is known as the *Horta d'Andratx* – the garden of Andratx. Even the Romans cultivated the land here and they founded the town as a center for this prosperous region, giving it the name *Andrachium*. Above all, wine, citrus fruit, almonds and olives are still harvested here.

The 13th-century **Parish Church of Santa Maria**, which was built like a fortress to resist pirate attacks, towers above the town.

SANT ELM

From Andratx, the PM-103 leads, via S'Arracó, to the relaxed fishing town **Sant Elm ⓭**. Sant Elm is an ideal choice for guests who wish to combine a beach vacation with hiking tours, and don't want to miss having the complete range of tourist entertainment in the vicinity.

Sant Elm is also a departure point for boat excursions to **Sa Dragonera ⓮**, an island nature reserve that measures four square kilometers in area (tours also leave from Port d'Andratx). It is also a departure point for tours to the watchtower **Cala Bassett** and the restored buildings of the former Trappist monastery of **Sa Trapa ⓯**. On this tour you have wonderful views of Sa Dragonera and the thickly forested southwestern tip of Mallorca.

ANDRATX
Bodega Santa Catarina, 4 km towards Capdella, tel: 971 235 413; excellent wine, free wine tasting on Sundays noon-2 pm.
Market Day: Wednesday.

ILLETES
O.I.T., Ctra. Andratx 33, tel: 971 402 739, fax: 971 405 444.
Riu Bonanza Park, Passeig de Illetes 8, tel: 971 401 112, fax: 971 403 362; base for guided walking tours that are organized by the Alpine School of Innsbruck.
Bon Sol, Passeig de Illetes 30, tel: 971 402 111, fax: 971 402 559; squash and tennis courts, children's playground, swimming pool.
Caves of Gènova, entrance at restaurant Ses Coves, tel: 971 402 387; April-Oct: daily 10 am-1:30 pm, 4-7 pm, closed Mon afternoon; Nov-March: daily 10 am-1 pm, 4-6 pm, closed Mon afternoon.

MAGALUF
O.I.T., Av. Pedro Vaquer Ramis 1, tel: 971 131 126, fax: 971 131 188.
BCM, Av. Olivera 14; Europe's largest disco with many attractions and up to 5000 dancers a night.
Palladium (casino), Urb. Sol de Mallorca.
Nemo Submarines (submarine trips), Av. P. Vaquer Ramis, tel: 971 130 227; operates March-Oct.
Golf Fantasia, C. Tenis 3, tel: 971 135 040; daily 10 am-midnight.

PALMANOVA
O.I.T., Passeig del Mar 13, tel: 971 682 365.
Port Orient, Passeig del Mar 8, tel: 971 682 829; good cuisine. Bodega Gloria Bendita, Passeig del Mar 18; excellent tapas bar.
Aquapark, Cami de Se Porrassa, tel: 971 130 811; March-Oct: daily 10 am-6 pm. Dorado City, near Aquapark, tel: 971 131 203; open nightly after 9 pm.

PEGUERA
O.I.T., Plaça Aparcaments 78, tel: 971 687 083, fax: 971 685 468.
Villamil, Av. de Peguera 66, tel: 971 686 050, fax: 971 686 815; castle-like building, directly on the beach, small indoor pool.
Phönix, Av. Peguera 7, tel: 971 687 724; was awarded the title of "Peguera's Most Beautiful Restaurant," creative cuisine. Ambassador, Sa Finca and Maloga, three of the better tourist-class restaurants on the main street. La Gran Tortuga, Urb. Aldea Cala Fornells 1, tel: 971 686 023; outstanding food, terrace

with sea view. **La Gritta**, C. L'Espiga 9, Cala Fornells, tel: 971 686 022; delicious shellfish, lovely view, try the grilled prawns.

Harry's Bar, C. Dragonern 1; music bar with live music daily, including jazz blues and folk.

PORT D'ANDRATX

O.I.T., C. Sa Fabrica 12, tel: 971 671 300.

Villa Italia, Camino de San Carlos 13, tel: 971 674 011, fax: 971 673 350; luxury lodging on a hill overlooking the harbor of Port d'Andratx, panoramic views of the southwest of the island, only 16 rooms/suites in a former mansion. The hotel's private beach, a rocky plateau, is reached via flights of steps.

Hostal Res. Catalina Vera, C. Isaac Peral 63, tel: 971 671 918; quiet location, parallel to the promenade.

Miramar, Av. Mateu Bosch 22, at the harbor, tel: 971 671 617; very good fish restaurant, the perch in a salt crust is excellent. **Es Saluet**, at the harbor; good fish dishes, e.g., turbot in saffron. **Don Giovanni**, Av. Mateu Bosch 20, at the harbor, tel: 971 673 359; Italian restaurant, famous far and wide. **Casa Galicia**, C. Isaac Peral, tel: 971 671 338; finest Spanish cuisine, especially good shellfish. **El Coche**, Av. Mateu Bosch, at the harbor, tel: 971 671 976; the specialty here is fish in a salt crust. **La Llonja**, Av. Mateu Bosch 6, tel: 971 674 164; another recommended fish restaurant that has fresh shellfish on the menu. **Rocamar**, Almirante Riera Alemany 27, tel: 971 671 261; outstanding fish restaurant near the harbor. **El Patio**, on the country road from Andratx to Port d'Andratx, tel: 971 672 013; good restaurant with tables in a courtyard.

XY, Av. Mateu Bosch 3; cozy bar with international clientele, many ex-pat finca owners meet here. **L'Havanna**, Av. Riera Alemany; Carribean atmosphere, a good place to watch the town's nightlife.

Trekking trail or circular drive, with fine panoramic views, to Cap d'es Llamp (5 km). **Boat tours** to Dragonera.

PORTALS NOUS

Bendinat, C. Andre Ferret Sobral 1, tel: 971 675 725, fax: 971 677 276; small house, directly on the sea, private beach.

Wellies, famous café on the harbor promenade, tel: 971 676 444; the "in" meeting place of the yachting crowd, i.e., the beautiful and successful, who come to be seen. Modest guests walk, pretentious ones drive up in their Rolls Royce. **Bismarque**, Local 53, tel: 971 677 225; breakfast, light lunch menu, evenings international cuisine with Mediterranean flair, all at a high culinary standard. **Tristan**, Plaça del Puerto, tel: 971 675 547; two (Michelin) star restaurant, here the Munich chef

Gerhard Schwaiger cooks the finest of everything. **Esdi's**, Edificio Midjorn, Local 29, tel: 971 676 981; outstanding dishes for people of the world, or those who consider themselves such. **Flanigan**, on the harbor promenade, tel: 971 676 117; breakfast, daily lunch menu, evenings excellent, light Spanish cuisine.

Banderas, Local 79; popular bar for the rich and beautiful, frequently with live music. **Meyer Lansky's**, directly on the harbor, popular "in" pub for the yachting crowd, a good place to see and be seen.

Marineland, near Costa d'en Blanes on the road to Palmanova, tel: 971 675 125; April-Sept: daily 9:30 am-6 pm, Oct-March: daily 9:30 am-5 pm. Amusement park and marine zoo.

SANT ELM

Hostal Dragonera, C. Rey Jaume Primero 5, tel: 971 109 086, fax: 971 109 013; pleasant guesthouse that is good value for money.

Arlequin, Cala Es Cunills 14, tel: 971 239 150; wonderful view of Dragonera.

Ferry to **Dragonera**: on Tue, Thu, Sat and Sun ferries leave 4-7 times daily; Mon, Wed, Fri at least twice daily.

SANTA PONÇA

O.I.T., Via Puig de Galatzó, tel: 971 691 712, fax: 971 694 137.

Bahia del Sol, Av. Jaume I, 74; tel: 971 691 150, fax: 971 690 650; separated from the sea by a road, about 250 meters to the sandy beach, about 400 meters to the town center, children's pool, indoor pool, and a sauna.

Mesón del Mar, Av. del Rei Jaume I. 103, tel: 971 692 313; simple, but very good Spanish cuisine. Restaurant in **Club Náutico**, at the marina, tel: 971 690 311. **Amadeus**, C. Santa Ponça 4, Costa de la Calma, tel: 971 694 286; has two chefs from Innsbruck, therefore, as well as good international dishes with a Mediterranean flair, it also offers Austrian specialties. **El Ceibo**, C. Ramon de Montcada 32, tel: 971 694 036; excellent South American cuisine and wines.

Tropicana, Centro Comercial Verdemar; popular cocktail bar, drink in the company of numerous screaming and talking parrots.

S'ARRACÒ

La Tulipe, Plça Toledo 2, tel: 971 671 449; a must for lovers good Italian cuisine.

Bar Galerie S'Arracò, C. de Francia 89; has continually changing art exhibitions; the place where art connoisseurs can drink their cocktails in a culturally inspiring atmosphere.

CENTRAL TRAMUNTANA

SOUTHERN PANORAMIC ROAD
SA GRANJA MOUNTAIN ROAD –
LA RESERVA DE MALLORCA
VALLDEMOSSA
DEIÀ
SOUTHEASTERN TRAMUNTANA

Central Tramuntana

The tour along the panoramic road from Andratx, via Valldemossa, to Sóller, then from Sóller past Mallorca's highest mountains to Pollença, and finally to Cap de Formentor is an absolute must during a visit to Mallorca, even if the journey is often slow because of the innumerable rented cars, tourists buses and, on the mountainous stretches, the swarms of training cyclists. To really get the most out of the trip, you should plan to take at least three days: one for the southern section, one for the section from Sóller to Pollença, and one for the Cap de Formentor region.

THE **SOUTHERN PANORAMIC ROAD

A few kilometers after the pass **Coll de Sa Gramola**, near Punta de Sa Llova (343 meters), you get a first glimpse of the sea far below. After this point the road runs parallel to the coastline.

Estellencs

Six kilometers from the viewing point **Mirador Torre de Ricardo Roca** is **Estellencs ❶**, at the foot of Galatzó – at

Left: For Archduke Ludwig Salvator, the most beautiful house on Mallorca was Son Marroig.

1025 meters it is one of the eight peaks of the Tramuntana that are over 1000 meters high. Estellencs is a typical Mallorcan village, with its narrow alleys, old houses of gray-brown quarry stone that is left unplastered, and a somewhat somber atmosphere.

All of the buildings here have a defensive character, an indication that pirates held the island and its inhabitants in their power for centuries. Even the belfry of the town's 15th-century church was converted into a place of refuge. The village chronicles report several instances of pirate attacks. Below the village, terraced fields, with plantations of fruit and olive trees, spread down toward the sea.

Several kilometers beyond Estellencs you come to one of the most beautiful viewing points on the entire Tramuntana Coast, the **Torre de Ses Animes ❷**, which was in the possession of the Archduke Salvator during the 19th century. A short wooden bridge leads across to a freestanding rock upon which a watchtower stands. From the tower there is a sweeping view of the sea.

Banyalbufar

The road now leads past extensive cultivated terraces that were laid out as early as the Moorish era, and to the small vil-

lage of **Banyalbufar ❸**. For many hundreds of years wine was produced here, but after a mildew epidemic in the 1920s the farmers began cultivating tomatoes instead of grape vines. The juicy red fruit from Banyalbufar has an excellent taste and a good reputation on the island.

Banyalbufar has an atmosphere similar to that in Estellencs. The houses here are also defensively built from unplastered quarry stone. The village is the staring point for a pleasant and easy walking tour to the Mallorcan summer resort of **Port d'es Canonge**.

*SA GRANJA MOUNTAIN ROAD – LA RESERVA DE MALLORCA

From Banyalbufar the road now climbs through many switchbacks to **Coll de Sa Bastida** (295 meters) and joins the PM-

Above: Possibly the best viewing point on the west coast – Torre de Ses Animes. Right: A lace maker at the Sa Granja Country Estate demonstrates her skills.

112, which comes from Palma. After about two kilometers on this road you reach the parking lots that are laid out for the large crowds of tourists that visit the **★Sa Granja Country Estate ❹**. Here, better than almost everywhere else, you can find examples of the development of farming life on the island throughout the centuries. The lords of the large estate, with extensive lands, were fully independent and could produce everything they needed, including dye for coloring the linen that they wove themselves.

In 1968, the present owners began a comprehensive program of renovations and soon thereafter opened the grounds and buildings to the public.

You can participate in an interesting and informative tour, viewing not only the manor house with its Florentine and baroque furnishings, but also all of the workshops and stables. You can thus take a walk through the spinning weaving and dying shops, print and carpentry shops, through the wine cellar with a winepress, past a distillery, and through a variety of storage buildings. Along the way you can admire a heavy olive press and many other interesting things. On Wednesday and Friday afternoons there are also demonstrations of the various skills and a "Mallorcan festival," with traditional folk dances, games and music.

The narrow, but very scenic mountain road, via Calvià to Palma, climbs through many tight switchbacks to a pass, then leads down into the fertile valley of **Puigpunyent**. The farming village, set amidst olive groves and fruit plantations, has a parish church, *L'Asuncíon*, which is almost 800 years old. A few kilometers south of the village, on the eastern slopes of Puig de Galatzó, there is a privately managed nature park, **La Reserva de Mallorca ❺**. The area covers 25 hectares and is also known as the *Paraíso de Mallorca de Reserva Puig de Galatzó*. It is home to almost all of the island's indigenous plants, and a four-kilometer-long circular walking trail leads past all of the reserve's attractions, including 30 waterfalls, some of which are artificial.

Continuing along the Panoramic C-710 to Valldemossa

From the junction to Sa Granja, follow the C-710 in a northerly direction towards Sóller. The winding road leads up to **Coll de Claret**, at a height of 495 meters. Shortly after the pass you will see, situated just off the road, the viewing point **Mirador Son Oleza**.

The next exit leads down to the coast and to the tiny village of **Port de Valldemossa**. The road that leads there seems to hug the steep cliffs, and four hundred meters below you can see the small harbor around which, on the weekends, when many locals are also here, so many cars are parked that even turning around can be pretty tricky. Shortly after the exit you come to Valldemossa, which, especially in the early afternoons, is usually overrun with visitors.

Central Tramuntana

*VALLDEMOSSA

The pretty little mountain town of *Valldemossa ❻ – which consists of an upper and lower town – is in a sheltered location, in the center of a wide green valley, at the foot of the 1064-meter-high Teix. Fruit and vegetables are cultivated on the terraced fields that spread out around Mallorca's best-known town. The imposing massif of the mountain Teix watches over what was once the love nest of two people without whom the cultural history of Central Europe would be unimaginable. In 1838/39, the French Baroness Dupin-Dudevant, better known by her pseudonym, George Sand, and the Polish composer Frédéric Chopin spent the winter in Valldemossa's **Carthusian Monastery** *Cartoixa de Jesús Nazareno*. That the two, who were unmarried and were therefore, in the moral understanding of the time, living in sin, happened to choose a monastery for their love retreat, gives the matter a certain piquancy. In her book *Winter on Majorca*,

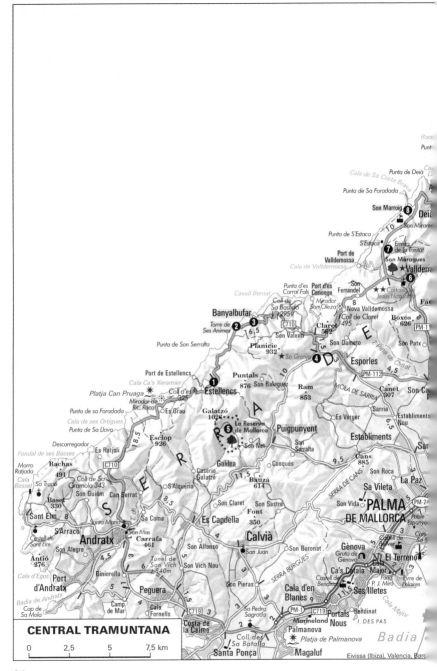

CENTRAL TRAMUNTANA

0   2,5   5   7,5 km

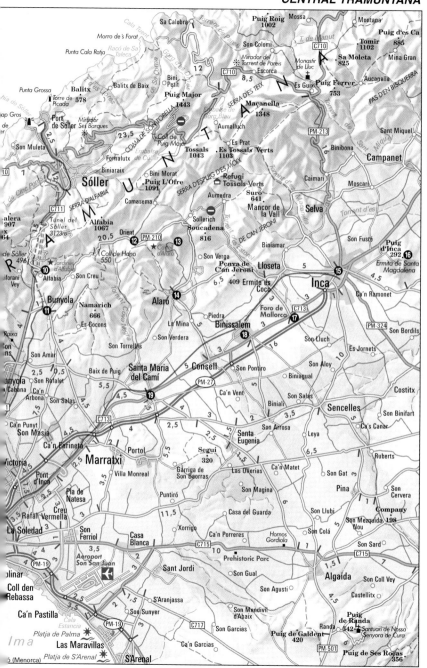

George Sand has left a detailed description of her experiences.

The **Charterhouse**, which was built in a former Moorish Alcázar complex during the 15th century, is located in a terraced garden from which there is a lovely view of the town and the surrounding countryside. Attached to the complex is a church with an adjoining monastery and the Palacio del Rey Sancho.

Visitors enter the grounds through the **abbey church**, which was begun in the neoclassical style in 1751 and was dedicated in 1812. The interior is decorated with stucco work, and one of the many statues shows Catalina Thomás who was born in Valldemossa in 1531, and was later canonized. She is still held in great reverence by the Mallorcans.

From the church you can enter the cloister and the monastery's historical **pharmacy**, which dates from the 18th century and is equipped in the typical manner of those times: ceramic and glass vessels, pestle and mortar, scales, pill crushers and retorts.

In the **library**, which adjoins the living quarters and private chapel of the prior, the monks used to assemble once a week – this was the only place in which their vows of silence could be broken. Books and manuscripts of the Carthusians, as well as an ivory triptych (15th century) complete the furnishings.

Some original letters from Chopin have been preserved in **Cell No. 2**, and there is also the old, out-of-tune piano at which Chopin worked on some of his compositions. In the glass showcases there are some of the master's original scores, an ivory comb, a jewel case, a lock of hair and albums with drawings and watercolors by Maurice Sand, the baroness' son. You may also admire the handwritten manuscript of *Winter on Majorca* and copies of the three first original editions of the book that were published in 1841, 1842 and 1855.

Cell No. 4 contains further mementoes of the master musician, such as the Pleyel grand piano at which Chopin composed the famous "Raindrop Prelude" (op. 28), and other well-known pieces. In another nearby room you can see Chopin's death mask.

Chopin and George Sand were by no means happy during their stay on Mallorca. George Sand suffered from the hostility of the locals towards her and longed for the luxury of Paris. Chopin had tuberculosis and his health deteriorated due to living under the monastery's damp vaults. One can imagine how relieved they both must have been when, after a long winter, they were able to return to Paris in the spring of 1839.

Every August an international Chopin Festival is held in Valldemossa's monastery, and it attracts famous pianists from all over the world.

The **Municipal Museum** *(Museu Municipal)*, which is also located in a section of the monastery, exhibits an old printing press from the Guasp printing works, which was founded in Palma in 1579. Another department deals with the activities of Austrian Archduke Ludwig Salvator while he was on Mallorca. Art also has also been included in these interesting exhibition rooms. The painting gallery, The Tramuntana Mountains, exhibits works by Mallorcan and Spanish painters who have found inspiration in the Tramuntana massif from the end of the 19th century onwards.

During the tourist season short piano concerts for visitors take place daily (included in the entrance fee) in the **King's Palace** *(Palau del Rei Sanç)*, opposite the monastery.

The **lower village** of Valldemossa is quieter and has much more atmosphere. The small, colorful houses nestle around

Right: During the winter of 1838/39, Chopin composed his Raindrop Prelude (op. 28) and other works in this cell at the former Carthusian monastery in Valldemossa.

the majestic parish church of **Sant Bartomeu**, which is mentioned for the first time in the annals of 1245.

The interior of the church is entirely devoted to the local saint, Catalina Thomás. Her modest house in the the Carrer de la Rectoria, in which she was born in 1531, has also been turned into a small chapel. Every year on July 28, the village celebrates the festival of its patron. The streets are decorated with garlands and a young girl from the village plays the role of Catalina.

Valldemossa is the starting point for a very lovely, walking tour of medium difficulty through the Son Moragues Nature Park and to two mountain peaks that offer excellent views.

Son Miramar and Son Marroig

Beyond Valldemossa and towards Sóller, the C-710 climbs slopes that are up to 400-meters-above-the-sea to the restaurant *Ses Pites*. From here take a narrow road that leads to the **Ermita de la Trinitat ❼**. Under large old trees there are some stone tables for pilgrims, at which, today, mostly Mallorcan families eat their picnics and enjoy the view of the rocky coastline and the sea with its breakers far below.

As you travel on, a short distance later you will see the white crenellated country estate of **S'Estaca**, which Archduke Ludwig Salvator had built for his life companion, Catalina Homar. You can also see the little palace **Son Miramar**, which was the main residence of the Archduke until the outbreak of World War I. Both of these buildings are now privately owned and are not open to visitors.

Continuing along the road to Deià, you pass on the right-hand-side the spring **Sa Font Figuera**, where Mallorcans like to fill water containers with clear mountain water. Shortly afterwards you come to **Son Marroig ❽**, another residence of the noble "drop-out." The once fortified finca has many exhibits that are reminders of the life and works of the Archduke. You can visit many of the rooms that have

been maintained in their original condition, and the view of the steep coastline from the rooms and balconies is one of incomparable beauty.

Below the square fortified tower is a path that leads to the **Punta de Sa Foradada**, a rock that points like a finger into the sea. The name, which means "holed through," originated from the hole, measuring almost 20 meters, which goes right through the hill.

DEIÀ

Past Son Marroig the panoramic road leads past the **Mirador de Sa Foradada**, then turns inland with a sharp bend and comes to the village of **Deià ⑨**. Generally known as an artists' village, it seems to be perched high above the sea on a mountain peak. Even with its many lovingly restored and converted houses, most of which were built in the 16th and

Above: Deià – a place of retreat for well-heeled artists.

17th centuries, it is plainly evident that the old buildings were originally built with defensive purposes in mind, and today, without exception, they still reflect the old fear of the pirate raids. This most attractive village has buildings that are decorated with flowers, steep narrow streets, flights of steps, simple and expensive restaurants, cafés, galleries and colorful pictures of the Passion of Christ on house walls. At the highest point of the village is the **Parish Church of Sant Joan Baptista**.

Beside the church is the cemetery. This is the last resting place of the English author Robert Ranke-Graves (1895-1985). His simple gravestone bears just three simple words: *Robert Graves – Poeta*. Graves spent almost 50 years of his life in Deià and laid the basis for the town's worldwide reputation. He was followed here by other writers and artists, including, for example, the German painter Ulrich Lehmann (1885-1987), the American artist William Walden, and the Austrian writer Jakov Lind. It the meantime,

Deià has become anything but an artists' village – today most of the houses are owned by moneyed aristocracy.

Graves came to Deià in 1929 and, with the exception of the years during the Spanish Civil War and World War II, he spent the rest of his life in this little mountain village. In 1968, the locals made him an honorary citizen. Graves achieved real fame only after the very long, but excellent film version of his book *I, Claudius* was shown on television. Another of his books, *Stories from the Other Mallorca*, is based on his experiences on the island.

The filming of an early-evening German television series, *Hotel Paradies*, in Deià's luxury hotel *La Residencia* has drawn an increasing number of bus tours to the village.

Continuing along the Panoramic Road

The road to Sóller skirts around Deià, turns again towards the sea, and leads past fields of gnarled old olive trees. The views along the way are wonderful. Then it passes the picturesque hamlet of **Lluc Alcari** and winds its way, with many curves, into a fertile valley basin behind which Mallorca's highest mountain, the majestic Puig Major, rises to a height of 1443 meters. In the curve of the valley lies the town **Sóller** (see p. 47). From here you can either continue the tour along the ****Northern Panoramic Road** (see p. 49) or take the quickest route back to Palma through the three-kilometer-long tunnel that was opened in 1997.

SOUTHEASTERN TRAMUNTANA

The *Gardens of Alfabia

Located near the southern entrance to the tunnel on the Palma to Sóller road are the ***Gardens of Alfabia ❿** (*Jardins d'Alfabia*), known among connoisseurs as Mallorca's most beautiful subtropical

park. Arabian landscape gardeners have expressed something of their vision of paradise here. Fountains and pools, shady avenues, palm groves, orange plantations and flower beds have been combined to create a peaceful oasis of relaxation. The old Arabian mansion exhibits furniture that is true to the original, large wall hangings, many paintings and a library. Upon leaving the estate you should take a glance upwards at the high ceiling of the tower over the entrance, which is adorned with precious inlaid work in the best tradition of the Almohade craftsmen.

Bunyola and Orient

From the *Jardins d'Alfabia* and the country estate Raixa, it is only a few kilometers to **Bunyola ⓫**, a pretty mountain village with a shady avenue of plane trees. It is home to Malloca's most famous palo distillery and has a typical village square in front of the church of Sant Mateu. The pride of the village's religious inhabitants is a 14th-century alabaster statue of the Virgin Mary. The "Red Lightning" train, which runs several times daily between Palma and Sóller, stops in Bunyola.

The journey along the PM-210 from Bunyola, via Orient, to Alaró is scenically very attractive, but because of its many curves, it takes considerably longer than the route via Santa Maria del Camí, which is just a little shorter in distance.

After Bunyola the road winds it way up through the **Coll de Hono** (550 meters) to **Orient ⓬**, which, because of its beautiful views, is regarded as one of the island's most charming mountain villages. Alleys with of flights of steps, about 40 houses, lots of flair and two fine small restaurants are all this little village has to offer.

Alaró

Southeast of Orient, after about 10 kilometers of scenic road – just past the

Central Tramuntana

★**Castell d'Alaro ⓭**, which stands atop a 750-meter-high vertical gray cliff, is the small town of **Alaró ⓮**.

Pleasant little Alaró, on the edge of the Tramuntana Mountains, has, as is quite common on Mallorca, a fortified church that is much too large for a town of this size. It was first mentioned in historical records in 1236. Next to the church is the town hall, built in the Renaissance style with arcades. Both buildings face onto the market place, which on Saturdays is full of hustle and bustle.

If you wish to visit the Castell d'Alaró, and are coming from the north, you don't even have to drive into town. Some distance before Alaró there are small signs for the exit to the fort, which can easily be missed. At first the narrow road runs between a quarry's high stone walls. When you come to the country estate *Son Penyaflor* you have to get out and open a cattle gate. A narrow gravel trail, which is signed, curves steeply past terraced olive groves and up to the fort. At the country restaurant *Es Verger* you can park and get something to eat – all the while enjoying the wonderful background of mountain scenery.

A steep path with many steps leads from the restaurant up to the plateau and the fort's ruins. The ascent takes about 45 minutes. From here you can continue on to the 822-meter-high peak, which offers a marvelous view – to the south as far as the Bay of Palma, to the east over the central plane Sa Pla, and to the north you can see the dominant massifs of the Puia Major and the Maçanella, Mallorca's highest mountains.

More than once the fort played a major role in Mallorca's history, and the fortified building was considered to be impenetrable. Early on, the Arabs recognized the strategic position and were the first to build a fort on this site.

Right: Meadows filled with flowers near Santa Maria del Camí.

After the invasion of the Christian armies, the scattered Moorish soldiers barricaded themselves in Alaró's fort, but they were forced to admit that their situation was hopeless and, in 1231, they surrendered the fort to James I without a struggle.

A horrible event took place here some decades later. During the conflict with the Kingdom of Aragón, Alfons III took over the island for a short period in 1285. King James II happened to be away from the island and his loyal followers occupied the fort and poured contempt on the Aragons' futile efforts to capture them.

Two of the Mallorcan leaders, Guillem Cabrit and Guillem Bassa, sent a message to Alfons' negotiators to the effect that they had never heard of a King Alfons, but only of *anfons* (halibut), which is eaten with sauce. The scorned Alfons promised bitter revenge, continued the siege despite great losses, and was finally able to capture the fort. In a play on the names of the Mallorcan leaders Cabrit and Bassa, he had the two men impaled on a stake and roasted alive on a spit. *Cabrit* means billy goat and Bassa sounds like *basa* (charcoal). The Pope subsequently excommunicated Alfons for this repulsive act. Thereafter, the local people honored the two courageous Mallorcans as martyrs. Urns containing their ashes are kept in the cathedral in Palma, and one rib from each man was kept – so tradition has it – in Alaró. The precious relics are preserved in a room in the small chapel of **Nostra Senyora del Refugi**, which was built in 1622.

You can spend the night in a small inn (with a restaurant) that is nearby.

Inca and Ermita de Santa Magdalena

Inca ⓯ is one of Mallorca's oldest settlements. The Romans maintained a stage and a resting place here on the road from Palma to Pollença. During the Moorish

era the town became the center of the fertile region around it and remained so after the *Reconquista*. Today, Inca has 20,000 inhabitants and is the third-largest town on Mallorca, after Palma and Manacor.

"Inca – the leather town," is what the billboards promise long before you reach the city limits, and the plentiful choice of goods that are available here attracts many tourists who come by the busload and in caravans of rented cars. The large leather-working companies have all established their associated sales rooms on the outskirts of the town.

Thursday is market day and, of course, leather products are also the main attraction here. There are also souvenirs and trinkets of all varieties. The market is purely aimed at visitors, so everything that could conceivably appeal to curious tourists is on offer.

After all of this shopping, people generally like to visit the *cellers*, basement restaurants, which grew out of former wine cellars and are known for their local atmosphere. Their rustic charm consists of old wine vats, rough wooden tables and high vaulted ceilings. One of the best of these restaurants is, without doubt, the *Celler Ca'n Amer*, in which good, traditional Mallorcan cuisine is served without modern embellishments.

As you follow the C-713 towards Alcúdia another road leads off to the right at kilometer marker 32. From here you climb up the slopes of the Puig d'Inca, around many serpentine bends and to the hermitage of **Ermita de Santa Magdalena** ⑯, which is still home to a few monks. There may have been a chapel as early as the time of the Moors on this 292-meter-high peak, but the first mention in the historical records of a chapel on this site dates from 1284.

Foro de Mallorca and Binissalem

Follow the C-713 towards Palma and shortly before you come to Binissalem you first pass **Foro de Mallorca** ⑰, which, despite of its appearance, does not really have any genuine medieval fortified buildings. It is only a sham backdrop for an amusement park. The nearby **wax museum** (*Museo de Cera*) records and displays Mallorca's most important historical developments along with its the island's most famous actors, most of which are now covered with patina.

Binissalem ⓲ can look back on a long history, and the name indicates a Moorish settlement from the 11th century. James II gave Binissalem its charter as a Christian city around 1300. And the Archduke Ludwig Salvator wrote of the excellent wine, "that is produced in the region in large quantities and must be counted among the best varieties of Mallorca, indeed of all the Balearic Islands."

If you would like to find out more about Mallorcan wine, you should pay a visit to the *Bodega José Ferrer*, on the main road, which is one of Mallorca's best. The *Bodega Antonia Nadal Ros*, in the finca San Roig, also enjoys a good reputation far and wide.

Santa Maria del Camí

The Romans very probably founded a resting post here on the road connecting Palma and Pollença, which in later centuries was further improved by the Moors. Today **Santa Maria del Camí** ⓳ has a busy leather and textile manufacturing industry. From quite a distance away you can see the fancy tiled roof of the baroque belfry of the **Parish Church of Santa Maria del Camí**.

Once you reach the center of town, the main street widens into a small square that is worth visiting, just to take a look. At house no. 31, the inscription *Nuestra Señora de la Soledad Can Cortrado* marks the entrance to the cloister of the former **Minorite Monastery**. The inner-courtyard is now overgrown with plants, but it is full of atmosphere. The **Museu Mallorqui** is located here and it offers visitors an exhibition of a variety of hand-crafted articles.

ALARÓ

🛏 🟢 **Nostra Senyora del Refugi**, near the Castell d'Alaró, tel: 971 510 480 and 971 182 112; simple accommodation in attractive surroundings.
❌ **Es Verger**, on the trail leading up to the Castell d'Alaró, tel: 971 182 126; not cheap, but try the shoulder of lamb.

BANYALBUFAR

🛏 🟢 **Sa Baronia**, right on the edge of town (coming from Andratx), tel/fax: 971 618 146; simple, but atmospheric hotel in an old nobleman's palace. **Hostal Ca'n Busquets**, C. Miramar 24, tel/fax: 971 618 213; small guesthouse, simple and stylish furnishing, with every necessary comfort.
❌ **Son Tomas**, C. Baronia 17, tel: 971 618 149; simple Mallorcan cuisine, marvelous view of the terraced fields of Tramuntana and the sea from the restaurant terrace. **Café Bellavista**, located on the village's main street, C. Conde de Sallet 11, tel: 971 618 004; light snacks, pretty view.

BINISSALEM

🛏 🟢🟢 **Scott's Hotel**, Plaça Inglesia 12, tel: 971 870 100, fax: 971 870 267; has an interesting Mallorcan-British hotel ambience.
❌ **El Suizo**, C. Pou Bo 20, tel: 971 870 076; best restaurant in town, large selection of Spanish wines. **Bodega Binissalem**, C. Foncs 51, tel: 971 468 764; an absolute must for wine-lovers.
🏛 **Foro de Mallorca** and **Museo de Cera**, tel: 971 511 228; daily 9 am-7 pm, in the winter only until 6 pm.
🛒 **Market Day**: Friday. **Bodega José Ferrer**, C. Conquistador 75; the area's largest wine producer. **Bodega Antonia Nadal Ros.**, in the Finca San Roig.
🍷 **Wine Harvest Festival**: on the 4th Sunday in September.

BUNYOLA

❌ **Sa Costa**, Costa de Sestacio 21, tel: 971 613 110; fine Spanish and international cuisine, mountain view.
🏛 **Gardens von Alfabia**, Mon-Fri 9:30 am-6:30 pm, in the winter till 5:30 pm, Sat 10 am-2:30 pm, closed Sun. **Country Estate Raixa**, tel: 971 790 379; Wed-Sun 11 am-7 pm, closed Mon and Tue.

DEIÀ

🛏 🟢🟢🟢 **La Residencia**, C. Son Canals, tel: 971 639 011, fax: 971 639 370; elegant hotel in a vine-covered mansion. **Es Moli**, Ctra. Valldemossa a Deià, tel: 971 639 000, fax: 971 639 333; luxury hotel in an old finca, with pool of spring water and view of the rocky coast.

⊖ **Pension Villa Verde**, C. Ramón Llull 19, tel: 971 639 037, fax: 971 639 485; pretty, comfortable guesthouse in a town house.

✖ **El Olivo**, in the classy La Residencia hotel, tel: 971 639 392; one of the island's best restaurants. **Sebastian**, C. Felipe Bauza, tel: 971 639 417; excellent food, the homemade ravioli with lobster and green asparagus is a hit. **Jaime**, on the main road Via A. Luis Salvador, tel: 971 639 029; simple restaurant serving Mallorcan cuisine. **Bodega Terraza**, on edge of town, coming from Valldemossa, pleasant restaurant on a quiet hillside.

ESPORLES – SA GRANJA

⊟ ⊖⊖ **Posada del Marques**, 5 km above Esporles, Urb. Es Verger, tel: 971 611 230, fax: 971 611 213; old finca, good view, stylish rooms, outstanding restaurant.

🏛 **Country Estate Sa Granja**, tel: 971 619 328; daily, 10 am-6 pm. Restaurant attached, tel: 971 610 655.

ESTELLENCS

⊟ ⊖ **Maristel**, C. Eusebio Pascual 10, tel: 971 618 529, fax: 971 618 511; simple establishment, good starting point for walking tours.

✖ **Son Llarg**, tel: 971 618 564, and **Montimar**, tel: 971 618 576, both on the Plaça Constitució; simple restaurants serving traditional Mallorcan food.

INCA

⊟ ⊖⊖⊖ **Casa del Virrey**, Ctra. Inca–Sencelles at km 2.4, tel: 971 881 018, fax: 971 883 323; hotel in the former residence of the viceroy, with a very good restaurant, quiet, located outside of town, only 16 rooms, pool.

⊖⊖ **Son Vivot**, Ctra. Inca–Alcúdia at km 34, tel/fax: 971 880 124; very nice rooms in a 12th-century country estate, with restaurant.

✖ **Celler Ca'n Amer**, C. de la Pau 39, tel: 971 501 261; the best basement restaurant in Inca, substantial Mallorcan cuisine in a rustic atmosphere. **Sa Travessa**, C. de la Pau; basement restaurant, popular with tourists. **Celler Ca'n Ripoll**, C. Jaume Armengol 4, tel: 971 500 024; good basement restaurant.

🛒 **Market Day**: Thursday.

🎪 **Agricultural Fair**: Dijous Bou, 3rd Thursday in Nov.

ORIENT

⊟ ⊖⊖ **L'Hermitage**, a little outside Orient on the PM-210, tel: 971 180 303, fax: 971 180 411; outstanding establishment, away from mass tourism, in an old abbey.

⊖ **Hostal de Muntanya**, in town center, tel: 971 615 373; guesthouse with 13 rooms.

✖ **Hostal de Muntanya**, on the main street, good suckling pig. **Mandala**, C. Nueva 1, tel: 971 615 285; on the steps leading up to the church, international cuisine.

PUIGPUNYENT

⊟ ⊖⊖⊖ **Gran Hotel Son Net**, at km 14 (coming from Palma) on the Palma road, tel: 971 147 000, fax: 971 147 001; newly reopened, one of the most magnificent fincas of the island, prices up to US $600 per night.

✖ **Son Gual**, at km 6 on the road to Palma, tel: 971 790 205; popular day-trip destination, on a small hill, Spanish specialties, adjoining riding stables. **Sa Taverna de Son Net**, in the Gran Hotel, imaginative cuisine by star chef Thierry Buffeteau, reasonable prices.

🏛 **La Reserva de Mallorca**, Wed-Sun 10 am-8 pm, in the winter only till 6 pm, closed Mon and Tue.

SANTA MARIA DEL CAMÍ

⊟ ⊖⊖⊖ **Read's**, see Info box on p. 24. **Finca Can Verderol**, Santa Maria-Ctra. A Portol, tel/fax: 971 621 204; country house with 10 rooms, which vary in quality, pool in attractive garden.

✖ **Celler Sa Font**, Plaça Hostels 14, tel: 971 620 302; all kinds of delicious tapas.

🏛 **Museu Mallorqui**, Mon-Sat 4-7 pm, closed Sun.

SON MARROIG

⊟ ⊖⊖⊖ **Sa Pedrissa**, Ctra. Valldemossa–Deià at km 64.5, tel: 971 639 111, fax: 971 639 456; first-class hotel.

🏛 **Finca of Ludwig Salvator**, Mon-Sat 9:30 am-2 pm and 3-7 pm, in the winter only till 5:30 pm, closed Sun.

VALLDEMOSSA

ℹ **O.I.T.**, Cartuja de Valldemossa, tel: 971 612 106.

⊟ ⊖⊖ **Vistamar**, Ctra. Valldemossa–Andratx at km 2, tel: 971 612 300, fax: 971 612 583; good hotel in former country estate, restaurant serving Mallorcan cuisine, elegant ambience. **Apartamentos El Encinar**, Ctra. Valldemossa, tel: 971 612 000, fax: 971 616 019; ca. 3 km outside Valldemossa on road towards Deià, car is essential for access.

⊖ **Hostal Ca'n Mario**, C. Uetam 8, tel: 971 612 122; simple accommodation, with restaurant, in town center.

✖ **Sa Cartoixa**, a few steps below the Carthusian monastery, tel: 971 612 240; one of the better addresses in town. **Ses Espigues**, C. Marques de Vivot, tel: 971 612 339; simple, good Mallorcan cuisine, unique kitschy atmosphere. **Ca'n Pedro**, Av. Lluis Salvador, tel: 971 612 170; rustic style, good food, fair prices. **Ses Pites**, between Valldemossa and Deià, tremendous view.

🏛 **Carthusian Monastery**, tel: 971 612 351. **Palacio del Rey Sancho** and **Museu Municipal**, Mon-Sat 9:30 am-1 pm and 5-6 pm, Sun 10 am-1 pm.

🎵 **Chopin Festival**: Sunday concerts in Aug and Sept, info at the Carthusian monastery. **Festival of Catalina Thomás**: on or around July 28.

THE NORTH

**SÓLLER / PORT DE SÓLLER
NORTHERN PANORAMIC ROAD
POLLENÇA
PORT DE POLLENÇA
FORMENTOR PENINSULA
ALCÚDIA / PORT D'ALCÚDIA
SOUTH OF ALCÚDIA**

SÓLLER

The majestic gray cliffs of the Puig L'Ofre (1091 meters) and the Puig Major (1443 meters) catch the rain clouds and thus ensure an abundance of water, which maks the valley basin around **Sóller ❶** Mallorca's most important fruit-growing region. Oranges, lemons, almonds, dates, apricots and figs all flourish here. In earlier times the Moors recognized the fertile conditions of the valley and named it *Suliar*, which roughly translated means, "valley of gold."

The museum train, "Red Lightning," runs six times daily between Palma and Sóller along a spectacular stretch of track that includes a total of 13 tunnels. The railway carriages were manufactured in England in 1912 and are of the finest workmanship – leather seats, leather baggage nets, brass fittings and mahogany paneling. And when you arrive at your destination in the little mountain town, the next railway wonder is awaiting your attention: a historical narrow-gauge streetcar.

From the railway station you are whisked along the streetcar tracks to the attractive **Plaça Constitució**, the square

Left: The second-largest canyon in the Mediterranean – the Torrent de Pareis.

in center of this bustling town. The large **Parish Church of Sant Bartomeu**, which was first mentioned in 1284, was constructed on the foundations of a former mosque. Its present-day form dates from the 16th century. Right beside it is the town hall, decorated with flags, which was built during the 17th century. Around the plaza, whose name of means "Constitution Square," are numerous cafés and simple restaurants with large shade trees.

The **Botanical Gardens**, which were laid out in 1992, together with the adjoining natural science museum **Museu Balear de Ciències Naturales**, should not be missed. More than 1700 species of trees, bushes and plants can be seen here.

*PORT DE SÓLLER

An ideal way to get to nearby harbor town of *Port de Sóller ❷ is by taking the nostalgic narrow-gauge streetcar, which first ran in 1913. It rattles along from Plaça Espanya, behind the church at the train station, and, making several stops along the way, reaches Port de Sóller in about 20 minutes. At the point where the little train leaves town there is a memorial to an event that is still actively commemorated by the *Moros i Christians*, a festival that is held every year on May 11.

The North

It was on this day in the year 1561 that a band of 1500 Moslem pirates appeared off the beach of Port de Sóller and began to raid the wealthy town of Sóller. In great haste the inhabitants of the town gathered together a voluntary force of 800 men, led only by two experienced soldiers. The battle went back and forth until the highly motivated local inhabitants finally succeeded in driving the pirates back into the sea.

The little town of Port de Sóller spreads picturesquely around a sweeping circular bay with a fishing port, a commercial harbor and a marina, as well as a little stretch of beach.

For a good view of the harbor and the town, you can go to either the lighthouse, **Cap Gros**, at the western end of the bay, or to the **Torre de Picada**, the former watchtower that is on the northern side. To reach the latter, built after the pirate raid in 1561, you have to cover the last

Above: It stands out among Mallorca's other mountain villages – the enchanting Fornalutx.

stretch on foot, which only takes about 15 minutes.

Fornalutx and Biniaraix

Just five kilometers east of Sóller is **Fornalutx** ❸, a charming little village that was founded by the Moors during the 12th century, and where it almost seems as if time has stood still ever since. Winding alleyways with flights of steps, narrow streets, fortified houses of quarry stone, colorful tile pictures on house walls, old arches, cobblestone paths, a shady plaza – complete with well and pail – and the old village church of Santa Maria; all these contribute to creating a unique atmosphere. It is little wonder that Fornalutx has been awarded the title of "Mallorca's Prettiest Village" a number of times.

The nearby village of **Biniaraix** ❹ is, in all these features, an equal. It too, is a settlement from Moorish times, and according to reliable sources, its name is a distortion of the Arabian *Beni A'rag*, which means approximately "sons of the lame one." Here you will find mostly the same collage of typical local features as is found in Fornalutx. Both of these villages lie at the foot of the 1091-meter-high L'Ofre, on the slopes of which, cultivated terraces yield fruitful harvests.

THE **NORTHERN PANORAMIC ROAD

The trip from Sóller to Pollença, via Lluc, is considered by many people to be even more impressive, more dramatic and more varied than the trip along the southern panoramic road. The **northern panoramic road** (C-710) also climbs to viewing points, many of them like eagles' eyries, where you can gaze down from giddy heights onto the waves breaking on the coast far below.

The next section of the tour is without a doubt one of the most beautiful in the northwest of the island. Again and again you can look down into valleys with their cultivated terraced slopes. Above everything towers the peak of the Puig Major, which at 1443 meters is Mallorca's highest mountain. At the highest point of the tour, **Coll de Puig Major** (1043 meters), the road leads through a narrow, pitch dark tunnel (watch out for cyclists!) to a Spanish air force base, from which a road that is closed to public traffic leads to the summit of the Puig Major.

In a deep valley, between the ridge of the Puig Major on one side and the Tossal (1043 meters) and Maçanella (1348 meters) on the other, there are two reservoirs, the Embalse de Cuber and Embalse de Gorg Blau, that play an important role in Palma's drinking water supply.

*Sa Calobra

The road known as *Sa Calobra ❺ is considered to be one of the most spectacular roads in all of Southern Europe. In a mere 12 kilometers it drops over 800 me-

ters. The name Sa Calobra means "the snake," and that is just what the road does – this imposing route winds like a snake along hairpin curves on artificially built ramps or narrow plateaus that have been widened. It is easily apparent that the engineer who built it, Antonio Paretti, thought carefully about the line of the road he was building. One curve is particularly ingenious in that the road doubles back 360° by passing under a bridge. It is claimed that he had the idea one morning while tying his tie and so the curve was named *Nus de la Corbata*, the "knot of a tie." While it was under construction more than 31,000 cubic meters of stones and rock were dug out by hand. Amazingly, no one now can remember why the road, built in 1932, was originally constructed.

After the road was completed, the tiny village of **Sa Calobra** grew up around the bay at its end. The bay has a stony beach, no swimming guests, empty restaurants and paths that are bereft of walkers. In fact, it is the quietest place on the island – in the evening, at night, in the early morning – until around eleven o'clock, or eleven thirty, when the invasion of tourist buses and rented cars begins. Tourists crowd the restaurants and push and shove their way through the narrow streets, looking for entertainment, souvenirs or a quiet place to watch the sea. By early afternoon, however, the noisy nightmare is over and Sa Calobra once again returns to its original tranquility.

*Torrent de Pareis

From the parking lot, a footpath leads through two narrow tunnels to the *Torrent de Pareis ❻, which plunges into the sea and, in the course of millions of years, has carved out of the rock the second largest canyon in the Mediterranean. Only experienced rock climbers should attempt a trek through this gorge, which involves an ascent of 620 meters. There

The North

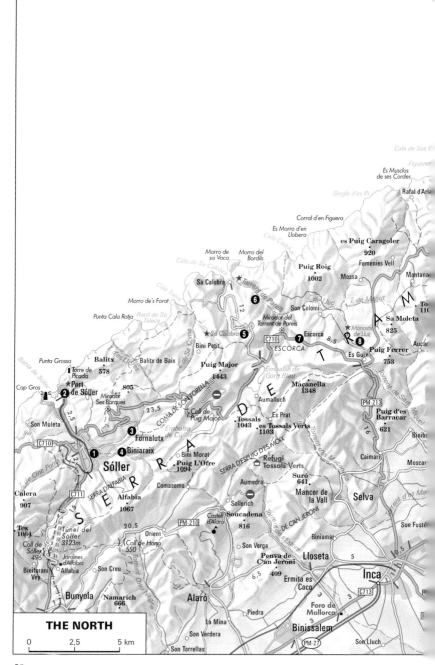

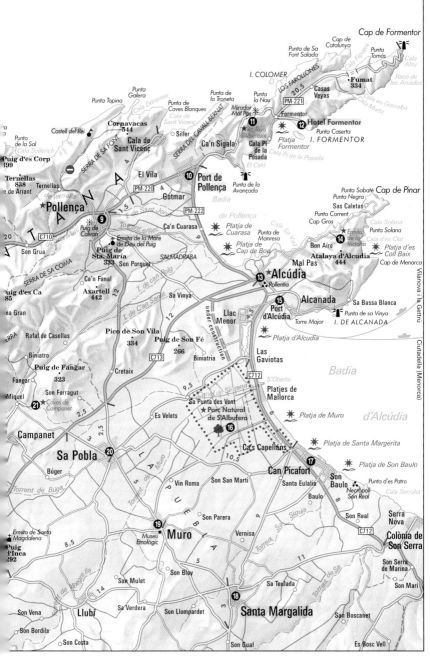

Cap de Formentor

Cap de Catalunya

Punta de Sa Font Salada

Punta Tomás

Cala Aloy

Racó de les Arcades

I. COLOMER

LOS FAROLLONES

20.5

Casas Veyas

•Fumat 334

Cala Figuera

Cala Murta

Cala en Gossalba

Punta Topina

Punta Galera

Cala Extremer

Punta de Coves Blanques

Cala de Sant Vicenç

Punta de la Troneta

Punta la Nau

Formentor

PM-221

Mirador Mal Pas ☀

11

Formentor

12 Hotel Formentor

Castell del Rei ♪

Cornavacas 544

•Siller

Ca'n Sigala

Atalaya d'Albercuix

Platja Formentor

Punta Caserta

I. FORMENTOR

Punta de la Sal

Cala Sollerich

Puig d'es Corp 899

Cala Pi de la Posada

El Caló

Cala Pi de la Posada

SERRA DEL CAVALL BERNAT

SERRA DE SA FONT

Ternellas 838

de Ariant

El Vila

PM-220

4

10 Port de Pollença

Punta de la Avançada

Punta Sabaté Cap de Pinar

Punta Negra

Sas Caletas

Cap de Pinar

Ternellas

de Ternella

★Pollença

Gotmar

PM-222

Badia

Punta Corrent

Cap Gros

Cala Solana

Ermita de la Victoria

Punta Solana

14

Cala d'es Clot

20

C710

9

Puig de Calvari ☀

Torrent de Sant Jordi

Ca'n Cuarasa

de Pollença

Cala Sant Vice

Platja de Cuarasa

Bon Aire

★Platja d'es Coll Baix

Son Grua

Torrent de Sant Mi

Ermita de la Mare de Deu del Puig

Puig de Sta. María 333

Son Porquet

S'ALMADRABA

Punta de Manresa

Platja de Cap de Bou

Punta de Sa

Mal Pas

Atalaya d'Alcúdia 444

Cap de Menorca

SERRA DE SA COMA

Ca'n Fanal

Axartell 442

13 ●Alcúdia

•Pollentia

uig d'es Ca 85

na Gran

12

T. de can Rolg

Sa Vinya

15 Port d'Alcúdia

Alcanada

Sa Bassa Blanca

Vilanova i la Gettru

RRA

Rafal de Casellas

Biniatro

Pico de Son Vila 334

Puig de Son Fé 266

T. de Can Sarret

12

Llac Menor

under construction

Torre Major

Punta de sa Vinya

I. DE ALCANADA

Ciutadella (Menorca)

Puig de Fangar 323

Cretaix

C713

Biniatria

Platja d'Alcudia

Fangar

Son Ferragut

21 ★Coves de Campanet

2.5

Es Velets

9.5

Canal de Siurana

S'Oberta

C712

Las Gaviotas

Badia

Miquel

Campanet

20

LA PUEBLA de sa Muro

2,5

Sa Punta des Vent

★Parc Natural de S'Albufera

16

Platjes de Mallorca

Platja de Muro

d'Alcúdia

Búger

5

10,5

Ca's Capellans

Platja de Santa Margerita

Sa Pobla

Torrent de Búger

Vin Roma

Son San Marti

17 Can Picafort

Santa Eulalia

Son Baulo

Platja de Son Baulo

Punta d'es Patro

Cala Serralot

Son Parera

Baulo

Necropoli Son Real

Ermita de Santa Magdalena

8,5

19 ●Muro

Museu Etnologic

Vernisa

Son Real

Serra Nova

Puig d'Inca 292

Torrent de Vinagrella

14

Son Blay

5

Siquia

C712

Colònia de Son Serra

Son Serra de Marina

Son Mulet

Sa Verdera

Son Llompardet

3

Sa Teulada

Torrent de Sa

11

Son Mari

Son Vena

Llubí

18

Santa Margalida

San Boscanet

Son Bordils

Son Costa

Son Gual

Es Bosc Vell

51

are signs along the way that warn of the strenuous route and its dangers. It may also only be attempted when the weather is good. When it rains, the gorge can fill with a raging torrent of water within minutes and can easily become a deadly trap. This warning also applies to taking the tour down the canyon, which begins at the parking lot of the restaurant *d'Escorca*, located a few kilometers further east on the C-710.

If you would prefer to avoid the mid-day hurly-burly of Sa Calobra and the beach section of the Torrent de Pareis, you can backtrack along the C-170 for about two kilometers, then turn right and follow the signs to the restaurant *Es Vergeret*. After about five kilometers you will reach the comparatively lonely town of **Cala Tuent**, which has a gravel beach and a good restaurant.

Above: Sa Calobra – like a snake, the road winds down the steep slopes. Right: A destination for many pilgrims, the "dark-skinned" Madonna.

*The Lluc Monastery

From the aqueduct it is a short drive to the **Mirador der Torrent de Pareis**, a point where you can look down into the canyon from a height of approximately 650 meters. Next you reach the little hamlet of **Escora** ❼ with its tiny church, *Sant Pere*, which is supposed to be the oldest chapel on the island.

For centuries the *Lluc Monastery ❽ has been Mallorca's most important place of pilgrimage, and as long as can be remembered it has been a place of veneration of the Virgin Mary. According to the tradition, after the *Reconquest* an Arab shepherd boy named Lluc found a statue of a dark-skinned Virgin Mary half buried in the ground. He brought it to the priest of Sant Pere, in Escorca, who placed the statue of the Madonna in his chapel. But the next morning it had vanished. It was found again exactly where Lluc had found it a day before and was returned to the chapel. Amazingly, this phenomenon occurred several times.

Entering through the main portal of the abbey, visitors find themselves in an inner courtyard in the baroque style, which has a memorial to the bishop Pere Joan Campins i Barceló, who rendered outstanding services to the monastery. The interior of the church receives little light, so it is difficult to adequately see the many frescoes and votive tablets. In a niche behind the main altar is the imposing statue of the Madonna – the main attraction for many reverent pilgrims and often less-reverent tourists.

Next to the church there is a small **museum** that displays finds from the Talayot culture. Several rooms are also devoted to contemporary works of the artist Coll Bardolet.

*POLLENÇA

The location of ***Pollença ❾**, in the center of a fertile, well developed area, surrounded by mountains, is as amazing as it is charming. The first settlement here, *Pollentia* (the mighty one), was founded by the Romans immediately after they conquered the island in 121 B.C. The origianal Pollentia was southeast of present-day Alcúdia, but after several Vandal plundering raids the inhabitants moved to this new Pollença, a little further inland at the Torrent de San Jordi. The **Roman bridge** dates from that time.

The center of town is the **Plaça Major**, which is lined with shade trees and cafés. Here too is the parish church of **Nostra Senyora dels Angels**, which was founded during the 13th century by the Knights of the Order of St. John of Malta. Further down from the Plaça is a former Dominican monastery, **Claustre del Convent Santo Domingo**, which today forms a stylish backdrop for the town's annual international music week.

Through a labyrinth of narrow alleyways that date from the Moorish period, you come to the **Town Hall**, located in part of the Monte Sión, a former Jesuit

monastery. To the left of the museum **Museu Martí Vicenç** (Mallorcan ceramics and fabrics), a flight 365 steps begins – one for each day of the year – and leads up to the 170-meter-high **Calvary Hill**. Along the Stations of the Cross, the *Via Crucis*, you will notice the crosses, each standing over three meters tall, that are 100 years old. At the top of the Puig del Calvari, the local mountain is crowned by a Neo-Gothic chapel in which you can see a statue of the "Mother of God at the Foot of the Cross."

South of town, the summit of the **Puig de Santa Maria** offers even better views across the island.

PORT DE POLLENÇA

The pleasant harbor town of **Port de Pollença ❿** is located where the sandy beaches of the wide, sweeping Bay of Pollença give way to the rocky cliffs of the Formentor Peninsula The bay, which is guarded by a fortress, the golden sandy beach, the palm trees along the attractive

The North

promenade, the hotels, which were not built too high, the barren, rocky mountains in the background – everything seems perfectly coordinated. Yachts bob up and down in the harbor and in the elegant restaurant of Club Náutico you can find a table with a great view.

Next to the marina there are several small boatyards, and then a long beach of fine sand. At the beginning of the 1990s the **Passeig vora Mar**, the new promenade and a pleasant, tree-lined place to stroll, was laid out along the beach.

A short time after World War II the Bay of Pollença was developed as one of the first tourist centers on the island. And since Winston Churchill used to spend his vacations in nearby Formentor, the location naturally became the favorite destination for great numbers of visitors from Great Britain – something that has not changed to this day.

Above: From a distance, the Formentor Peninsula looks rocky and inhospitable, but it has pretty bays that are suitable for swimming.

THE **FORMENTOR PENINSULA

You will find many attractive mountain roads with magnificent viewing points on Mallorca, but nowhere is nature so dramatic and threatening as it is in the steep cliffs of the **Formentor Peninsula**.

Antonio Paretti, the engineer responsible for Sa Calobra, was also in charge of the design of this road, which runs from Port de Pollença and along the long, narrow peninsula to the northernmost tip of Mallorca – **Cap de Formentor**. You come to the **Mirador Mal Pas**, the first viewing point, after six kilometers. A monument to the road's builder of the road was placed here – it is shaped like a bizarre rocky needle. A short paved footpath leads from the monument across the deeply furrowed chalk cliffs to the viewing point **Es Colomer**, where a fantastic view of the peninsula, which points out into the sea like a finger, opens out before you.

Opposite the parking lot a narrow winding road that leads to the peninsula's highest peak begins. This is where a 16th-century watchtower, the **★Atalaya d'Albercuix ⑪**, stands.

The road to the cape descends again towards the sea, to the exit for **Cala Pi de la Posada**. The shady beaches here, on the wooded, sheltered eastern side of the peninsula, are among the most beautiful on the island. At the northern end of the bay is Mallorca's most famous first-class hotel, the **Hotel Formentor ⑫**.

If you don't have a car you can get to Hotel Formentor's beach with an excursion boat from Port de Pollença, or with one of the many busses that run there several times a day, also leaving from Port de Pollença.

As you continue along the road to the cape, a short distance further on you will see the houses of **Casas Veyas**. A footpath leads from here to the isolated town of Cala Murta, to which few visitors stray, even in the peak season. Next you pass a memorial to the Mallorcan poet Miquel Costa i Llobera, which has been surrounded with a small garden.

The road then climbs through pine forests up to an unlit tunnel (watch out for cyclists!) through which you cross the peninsula for the third time. At kilometer 12 a you can head to **★Cala Figuera**, one of the island's prettiest swimming spots.

The road continues to swing from the east coast to the west coast of the narrow peninsula and the landscape becomes more barren and inhospitable.

The lighthouse at **★Cap de Formentor**, built in 1862, is located more than 200 meters above the sea. Its light is the strongest on the Balearic Islands – it is visible from over 60 kilometers away and can be clearly seen from nearby Menorca.

★ALCÚDIA

From Port de Pollença the PM-222 leads eight kilometers along the bay to **★Alcúdia ⑬**. As archeological findings have demonstrated, the region around Alcúdia was the part of the island that was first settled. To the west of the town, near the Roman amphitheater, are the remains of a prehistoric Talayot tower. The Romans, who sent out an invading fleet in 123 B.C., under the leadership of Quintus Caecilius Metellus, selected the sheltered bay with its flat sandy beach as a suitable landing place. Their punitive expedition had the aim of ridding the Mediterranean of the Mallorcan pirates once and for all. After their victorious battle, the new masters founded a city here that they called *Pollentia*, the "mighty one," and began to spread Roman culture extensively across the island.

After the Vandals burned the original settlement to the ground in A.D. 440, the Moors used the ruins of Pollentia as a "quarry" where they obtained stones for building their new settlement, **Al Kudia** (the hill). Because of this, there are very few remains left from the Roman period. The Arab settlement grew quickly and a harbor of strategic importance was built, however, it did not succeed in outstripping Palma to the south.

Around 1300, after successfully conquering the entire island, James II had a defensive city wall constructed as protection against the raids of the corsairs. The wall is still well preserved today.

If you drive along the city wall (parking lots), you will notice, at the exit to Can Picafort, the **Parish Church of Sant Jaume**, which is integrated into the defensive fortifications. The church dates from the middle of the 13th century, but was extensively altered 300 years later. Above the main portal there is a large, very beautifully worked rose window. The Gothic main altar in the interior has a portrait of the patron saint, after whom the church is named, and in a side chapel there is a large and impressive baroque altar with the "Cross of Christ of Alcúdia," about which many legends are told and which is carried through the streets every three years, on July 26, in a procession.

The North

You can enter the church's museum (*Museu Parroquial*) through the baroque side chapel. The museum's exhibits include old church vestments and liturgical articles.

The **Museu Monogràfic de Pollèntia** behind the church, displays vivid illustrations of life during Roman times, from the first century B.C. to the sixth century A.D.

At the eastern end of the town is the city gate, **Porta de Xara**, which is no longer part of the circular wall. Around this sprawls **Plaça de Carlos V**, the wide plaza with much greenery where a market is held on Tuesdays and Sundays. Today the market is geared more toward the interests of tourists than the requirements of the local people.

The **ruins of the Roman city of Pollentia** can be seen opposite the church of Sant Jaume and across the busy street. In the area that has to date been excavated

Above: A swimming bay at the resort of Bon Aire, near Alcúdia.

by archeologists, the course of the streets, foundation walls and individual columns have been uncovered. Signs direct visitors to the remains of a **Roman amphitheater**, of which part of the stage and the rows of seats have been preserved. The little Romanesque chapel of **Oratori de Santa Ana** dates from the early days of the *Reconquista* and was erected using stones from the Roman city.

*Ermita de la Victoria

Even those who have only a moderate interest in Mallorca's sacred architecture should take time to visit the hermitage of ***Ermita de la Victoria ⓮**, northeast of Alcúdia. The journey is also worthwhile because of the enchanting view, and some guests may come solely to eat in the excellent restaurant *Mirador de la Victoria*, located next to the hermitage. The road there leads through the resorts of Mal Pas and Bon Aire, with their many vacation homes, past a small marina, then winds upwards through a shady forest to quite an altitude. After about seven kilometers a dead end road, with more hairpin bends, leads to the Ermita, another typical Mallorcan place of veneration of the Virgin Mary.

Every year, two days after Easter, a festival, the *Pancaritat*, is held at the chapel, and every July 2 there is a pilgrimage to the chapel.

PORT D'ALCÚDIA

Port d'Alcúdia ⓫ was once nothing more than a sleepy fishing village. Today, however, it is a modern tourist center with three harbors: a marina, a fishing harbor and a commercial harbor where ferries from Menorca, excursion boats to the Formentor Peninsula, and large container ships dock.

From the harbor take the C-712 and head south along the curving bay. For more than 10 kilometers you will see row upon row of hotels, apartment buildings, vacation homes, shops and restaurants, one after another. The reason so many vacationers like to come here is hidden behind the hotels: a well cared-for beach with fine sand that reaches all the way to Can Picafort.

At the beach (Platja d'Alcúdia), the hotels are arrayed in a seamless line, starting at **Las Gaviotas**. Then the main road leading to Can Picafort crosses the Siurana Canal, where the trail to the S'Albufera Nature Park turns off, and finally reaches the beach **Platja de Muro**, where the pine forests stretch, in some places, right down to the beach.

SOUTH OF ALCÚDIA

*S'Albufera Nature Park

With an area of 2400 hectares, the region of *S'Albufera** ⓰ is Mallorca's largest wetland biotope, and almost 200 species of birds find refuge here. In the 17th and 18th centuries canals were built

to drain the region, in order to gain more land for agricultural purposes. The material that was excavated from these artificial waterways was spread out on square plots of land giving rise to fields that were always well supplied with water, the so-called *marjals*.

The project was so successful that, in the 19th century, a British company was commissioned to carry out further land reclamation on a large scale. Canals, with a total length of 400 kilometers, were dug and a pumping station lowered the water table by several meters.

The engineers, however, underestimated the power of the sea that seeped into the drained areas and generally made the new fields too salty for rice production. Since agriculture was no longer possible, a paper mill was built here and it operated until 1966. Today, the building is part of the Visitor's Center. In 1988, the Balearic Islands' regional government placed the entire wetland region under legal protection.

There are approximately 20 species of fish, including the common eel and perch, living in the labyrinthine system of canals and ditches. Frogs can be heard croaking everywhere and, if you are observant, it is very likely that you will be able to see some turtles.

It is the bird world, however, that has the widest range of species here, and the park's Information Center has listed all of the species that are represented. The list, available in English, includes the osprey, hawk eagle, purple heron and little egret, flamingos, many varieties of falcon and by far the largest population of nightingales in all of Europe.

The entrance to the Nature Park is next to the bridge on the C-712, opposite the newly built five-star Hotel Parc Natural. Since cars are not permitted and must be left at the Visitor's Center, the best way to explore the park is by bicycle. The Visitor's Center is located about 1.5 kilometers from the park entrance.

The North

The last town on the long sandy Bay of Alcúdia is **Can Picafort** ⑰. It has also developed from a small fishing village into a popular tourist center, but it is quieter and less expensive than Alcúdia.

Can Picafort is, like the other towns on the Bay of Alcúdia, an ideal starting point for cycling tours through the S'Albufera Nature Park and across the plain of **La Puebla**, which is dotted with numerous windmills.

If your schedule allows, you should also go to the little country town of **Santa Margalida** ⑱, which is most enjoyable in early September. This is when there is a festival, lasting several days, in honor of Saint Catalina Thomás (*Festes de la Beata*), in which the saint, who was born in Valldemossa, is celebrated with a colorful procession.

Those who are interested in the historical customs of Mallorcan festivals should not miss a trip to the noteworthy **Museu Etnològic** in **Muro** ⑲, which is just five kilometers to the northwest. Another village in the area that is worth mentioning is **Sa Pobla** ⑳, where there is a market on the central plaza every Sunday. There is also an interesting cemetery with an unusual number of large tombstones and the 14th-century parish church of Sant Antoni Abat.

★The Caves of Campanet

After about 14 kilometers on the busy Alcúdia to Palma road, there is an exit to the right that leads to the stalactite caves ★**Coves de Campanet** ㉑, which were first discovered in 1945. The passages in the caves are 1300 meters long and have a constant temperature of 18°C, in both the summer and the winter.

The cave's main attraction is in the *Sala Romantica*, about 50 meters underground. The "piece of cord" got its name because it is only five millimeters thick, which makes it the thinnest stalactite on record.

S'ALBUFERA AND SURROUNDINGS

S'Albufera Nature Park, April-Sept: daily 9 am-7 pm; Oct-March: daily 9 am-5 pm. Entrance near Hotel Parc Natural, at the sea.

Toni Cotxer in **Sa Pobla**, directly at the market, tel: 971 540 005; the spiciest tapas on the island.

Museu Etnològic in **Muro**, C. Major, tel: 971 717 540; Tue-Sat 10 am-2 pm and 4-7 pm, Sun 10 am-2 pm, closed Mon.

Festes de la Beata, in **Santa Margalida**: early Sept.

ALCÚDIA

Mirador de la Victoria, ca. 5 km from Alcúdia, tel: 971 547 173; great restaurant with a view. **Sa Plaça**, Plaça de la Constitució; small and simple.

Museu Monogràfic de Pollentia, C. Sant Jaume 30, tel: 971 547 004; Mon-Fri 10:30 am-1 pm, 3-6 pm, Sat & Sun 10:30 am-1:30 pm, shorter winter hours.

Market Days: Tuesday and Sunday.

Bullfighting Arena, Plaça des Toros; July & Aug.

CALA SANT VICENÇ

O.I.T., Plaça Cala Sant Vicenç, tel: 971 533 264.

Cala Sant Vicenç, C. Maressers 2, tel: 971 530 250, fax: 971 532 084; almost 40 rooms in superior country house-style, restaurant, central location.

CAN PICAFORT

O.I.T., Plaça Gabriel Roca 6, tel: 971 850 310, fax: 971 851 836.

Parc Natural, at the Platja de Muro, tel: 971 892 016, fax: 971 890345; opposite S'Albufera Nature Park. **Camping Club Picafort**, Ctra. Artà-Alcúdia at km 23.4, tel: 971 537 863, fax: 971 537 511; 1000 sites.

Solimar, near Colònia de Sant Pere, tel: 971 589 347; fine quality at high prices.

CAMPANET

Caves, daily 10 am-6 pm. **Glass Manufacturing** in the **Menestralia Mansion**, tel: 971 877 104.

FORRNALUTX

Hostal Fornalutx, C. de Alda 22, tel: 971 631 997, fax: 971635026; simple rustic style.

Bellavista, C. S. Bartolomé 30, tel: 971 631 590; simple restaurant with a fantastic view.

THE FORMENTOR PENINSULA

Formentor, Platja de Formentor, tel: 971 865 300, fax: 971 865 155; Mallorca's most famous luxury hotel, beautiful beach.

LLUC

📧 ⓢ **Lluc Monastery**, tel: 971 517 025, fax: 971 517 096; good value that is esp. appreciated by hikers.

❌ **Sa Fonda**, in the Lluc Monastery, tel: 971 517022. **Es Guix**, lies secluded on road to Inca, tel: 971 517092; inside local cuisine, outside picturesque pool of spring water.

🏛 **Lluc Monastery Museum**, daily 10 am-5:30 pm.

POLLENÇA

📧 ⓢ **Hostal Juma**, Plaça Major 9, tel: 971 533 258, fax: 971 534 155; only hotel in Pollença, simple yet very stylish, completely restored in1996.

❌ **Il Giardino**, Plaça Major, tel: 971 534 302; good Italian food. **Ca'n Costa**, C. Costa i Llobera 11, tel: 971 530 042; good wine menu, excellent food. **La Font del Gall**, C. Montesiön 4, tel: 971 530 396; good, small restaurant, French & Mallorcan menu. **La Fonda**, C. Antoni Maura 31, tel: 971 534 751; in a beautifully restored town house, outstanding Mallorcan cuisine.

🍽 **Café Espanyol**, directly on the Plaça Major 2; traditional café, practically an institution.

🏛 **Dominican Monastery** and small **Museum**, July-Sept: daily 10 am-1 pm and 5:30-8:30 pm, Oct-June: daily 11 am-1 pm. **Museu Martí Vicenç**, next to the town hall, below Calvary Hill, normal opening times.

🏷 **Vegetable Market**: Sundays on the Plaça Major.

🎵 **Festival Internacional de Música**: Aug and Sept.

🚌 **Banca March**, tel: 971 531 177.

PORT D'ALCÚDIA

ℹ️ **O.I.T.**, Mariners, tel: 971 547 257, and **O.I.T.**, Ctra. de Artà 68, tel/fax; 971 892 615.

🚢 **Ferries** to **Menorca** leave from the commercial harbor, tel: 971 549 442. Ferries to **Formentor Peninsula** leave from Passeig Maritimo, tel: 971 545 811.

📧 ⓢⓢ **Astoria Playa**, Av. de México 1, tel: 971 890 000, fax: 971 890 689; large pool area.

❌ **Miramar**, Paseo Maritimo 2, tel: 971 545293; founded in 1871, one of the best restaurants in town. **Bogavante**, C. Teodore Canet 2, tel: 971 547364; small, but cozy "lobster parlor."

🍽 **Menta**, Av. del Tucan, near the Hidroparc; largest and most famous disco in the entire area.

🚢 **Hidroparc**, Av. del Tucan, tel: 971 891672; daily 10 am-6 pm, large water park with slides and pools.

PORT DE POLLENÇA

ℹ️ **O.I.T.**, C. Juán XXIII. 46, tel/fax: 971 865467.

📧 ⓢⓢ **Uyal**, Passeig de Londres, tel: 971 865 500, fax: 971 865 513; near town, harbor and beach.

❌ **Club Náutico**, at the marina, tel: 971 865 622; one of the best restaurants in town. **Taverna Cap de Cantóc**,

C. Monges, tel: 971 866 103; good restaurant, delicious food. **Los Faroles**, Paseo Saralegui 64, tel: 971 866 863; very good fish restaurant, outstanding paella. **La Lonja**, Muelle Pesquero, tel: 971 532 077; pleasant fish restaurant on the harbor. **Stay**, at a harbor breakwater, tel: 971 864 013; fantastic Mediterranean and Mallorcan cuisine.

🍽 **Es Casinet**, Anglada Camarassa 15; night bar.

🚢 **Ferries** to **Formentor Peninsula**, June-Sept: 7 times daily, from the quay at the restaurant Stay.

PORT DE SÓLLER

ℹ️ **O.I.T.**, C. Almirante Miranda, tel: 971 633 042.

📧 ⓢ **Miramar**, C. Marina 12, tel: 971 631 350, fax: 971 632 671; inexpensive, good value, near the harbor and beach.

❌ **So'n Cora, El Pirata** and **Ca's Mariner**, all three on C. de Santa Catalina d'Alexandria, good to very good fish restaurants, at the harbor.

🚢 **Boat trips** to Sa Calobra, April-Oct: 3 times daily.

SA CALOBRA – TUENT

❌ **Es Vergeret**, Cala Tuent; fair prices, superb view.

🚢 **Boat trips** to Port de Sóller, April-Oct: 3 times daily.

SÓLLER

ℹ️ **O.I.T.**, Plaça Constitució 1, tel: 971 630 200.

📧 ⓢⓢ **Ca's Puers**, C. Isabell II 39, tel: 971 638 004, fax: 971 630 429; in an old town house in the center of Sóller, five rooms, two suites, every comfort, antique furnishings, outstanding restaurant of German master chef Roland Trettl. **Finca Ca N'Ai**, Cami de Son Sales 50, tel: 971 632 494, fax: 971 631 899; excellent address a little outside Sóller in an old country estate. **Ca'n Coll**, Cami de Ca'n Coll 1, tel: 971 633 244, fax: 971 631 905; stylish finca in large citrus grove.

ⓢ **Ca'n Roses**, C. de Quadrado 9, tel: 971 632 299, fax: 971 633 217; small city hotel, large garden, pool.

❌ **Bens D'Avall**,between Deià and Sóller, tel: 971 632 381; excellent value for money, top cuisine, wonderful view. **Ca's Puers**, C. Isabell II 39, tel: 971 638 004; best restaurant in town, fantastic view. **Ca's Carrete**, Plaça de America, tel: 971 630 364; popular with the locals, simple, but good food. **Sa Teulera**, C. Puig Major, tel: 971 631 111; roast suckling pig from the spit is the speciality here, guests can watch it roasting.

🏛 **Casa de Cultura**, Mon-Fri 11 am-1 pm and 5-8 pm, closed Sat and Sun. **Botanical Gardens – Museu Balearde Cièncas Naturales** (Balearic Science Museum) on the main road to Palma, tel: 971 634 064; Tue-Sat 10:30 am-1:30 pm and 5-8 pm, Sun 10:30 am-1:30 pm, closed Mon.

🎭 **Festes de Moros i Christians**, May 11.

The North

THE NORTHEAST

CALA RAJADA
CAPDEPERA
ARTÀ
ALONG THE COAST
THE INTERIOR

CALA RAJADA

This little fishing town at Mallorca's extreme northeastern tip has not entirely escaped the turbulent development that comes with tourism. It has, however, managed to retain a surprising amount of its Mediterranean charm. This has to do, largely, with the fact that **Cala Rajada ❶** is still a fully operative fishing port. Many *llaüts* and larger trawlers can be seen in the harbor basin, alongside sailing yachts and smart motorboats.

All around the harbor, on raised terraces, there are numerous small cafés and restaurants. This is a good place to drink a *café con leche* and to absorb the Mediterranean surroundings. It may be hard to believe, but Cala Rajada is the island's second largest fishing port, after Palma. This is mainly due to the area's rich prawn fishing grounds that are found off the coast.

Cala Rajada is on a little peninsula that reaches into the sea, and a long coastal promenade leads west from the sandy bay of **Cala Gat** in the southeast, past the harbor, to the beach of Son Moll. In the north the rocky Cala Lliteras is a favorite meeting place for divers, and a little further

Left: Northeastern Mallorca is a paradise for windsurfers.

west, the sun worshippers prefer the sandy beach, which is backed by pine trees, at **Cala Guya**, one of the island's most popular tourist spots.

Above the town, on what was the site of watchtower, you can find **Casa March**, the villa that the Mallorcan multimillionaire Joan March (1880-1962) built on this exposed location at the beginning of the 20th century. Joan March, who has been called the last pirate of the Balearics, began life as the impoverished son of a swineherd and became the richest man on Mallorca. He owed a large part of his wealth to his wheelings and dealings with the Mafia and illegal trade in cigarettes and weapons.

The villa is located in a park that covers an area of 60,000 square meters, in which more than 40 *★sculptures by renowned artists are displayed. Among others, there are works by Auguste Rodin and Henry Moore. Inside the house there are paintings by Picasso, Chagall and other classical Modernists. It is said that the villa is not lived in during most of the year and it is only occasionally, on guided tours organized by the local tourist office, that visitors get a chance to see the sculptures in the park.

You can walk from the beach at Cala Guya, over a wooded hill at the foot of the 272-meter-high Jaumell, and to the pretty

The Northeast

beach of **Cala Mezquida**, where you will find several simple restaurants. Nude tanning and swimming is allowed in some places in **Cala Torta**, the next bay over.

*CAPDEPERA

Just a few kilometers inland lies the pleasant little town of ***Capdepera ❷**, whose appearance is dominated from afar by a **fort** that stands proudly on the ridge of a hill and is extremely well preserved. The Romans probably maintained a defensive structure on this hill because of its favorable strategic position. The Moors made considerable additions to the fortress so that it was able to withstand both the *Reconquista* by the troops of James I, as well as the fierce pirate raids. Furthermore, a statue of the Madonna seemed to

Above: The lighthouse at Punta de Capdepera marks the easternmost point of the island. Right: Mallorca is one of the best places in Europe to golf. You can find good courses, like this one near Capdepera, everywhere.

bring the population added protection – at least this is what the old Mallorcan legends that were noted down by Archduke Ludwig Salvator relate.

According to one traditional tale, a troop of club-swinging pirates once landed in Cala Rajada and headed towards Capdepera. The people of the town implored the Madonna to help them and as soon as the first fervent words were spoken a thick fog rose up. The corsairs lost their orientation and with some difficulty they made their way back to their boats and sailed away without achieving their aim. From that time on their statue of Mary was known to the inhabitants of Capdepera as *Sa Esperança*, "Bringer of Hope."

In the following centuries, the *Virgen de la Esperança* must also have held her protecting hands over the town, which was particularly at risk because of its location so near the coast. As a result of this protection, today's visitors can inspect one of the best-preserved medieval fortresses on Mallorca.

The Northeast

*ARTÀ

If you travel another eight kilometers inland from Capdepera, you can see from a distance a large parish church and above it the church of Sant Salvador, a striking symbol that is built like a fortress. Both of these belong to the town of *Artà ❸.

The **Plaça Espanya**, with its many palm trees, is the center of town. Also here are the **Town Hall** and the **Museu Regional**, which exhibits archeological finds from the region. It is an ideal starting point for a short walk along the Way of the Cross, up to the pilgrimage chapel.

The massive **Parish Church of Transfiguració del Senyor** was built on the foundations of the town's former mosque. Because of the long years of danger from pirates, the church was reinforced for defensive purposes. Inside, the carved pulpit is of special interest.

A path made of steps and lined by cypress trees, with attractive stone Stations of the Cross, leads uphill to Artà's fortress. Over the crenellated parapet of the terrace there is a marvelous view of the town and the fertile region around it. There is also a view of Capdepera's large **fort** and, behind it, the coast. The simple present-day form of the *Pilgrimage Church of Sant Salvador**, which is surrounded by the fortifications, dates from the early 19th century. The church houses many valuable paintings, of which two illustrate the history of Mallorca and are of particular cultural importance. Just to the right of the entrance is a picture of the defeated Moorish Emir, as he hands over his kingdom to James I. To the left, there is a picture of the stoning of the saint Ramón Llull in North Africa.

On the main road leading through the town, a sign directs you to the ruins of *Talayot des Ses Paises ❹**, which, along with those of Capocorp Vell, represent the most significant remains of prehistoric settlements on Mallorca. An impressive defensive wall, about two meters in height and composed of large, square stone blocks, give you an idea of the large dimensions of this megalithic settlement.

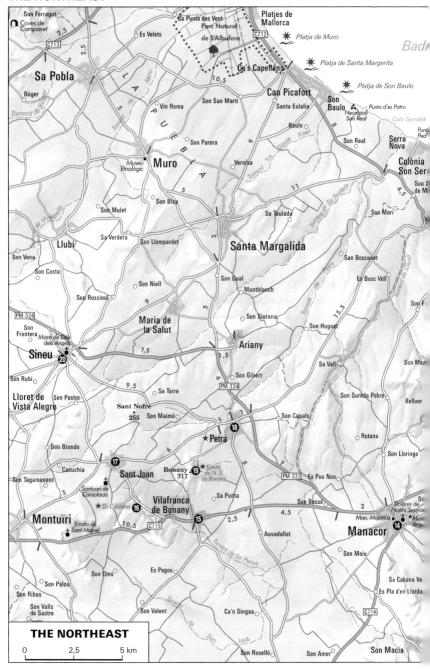

THE NORTHEAST

0   2,5   5 km

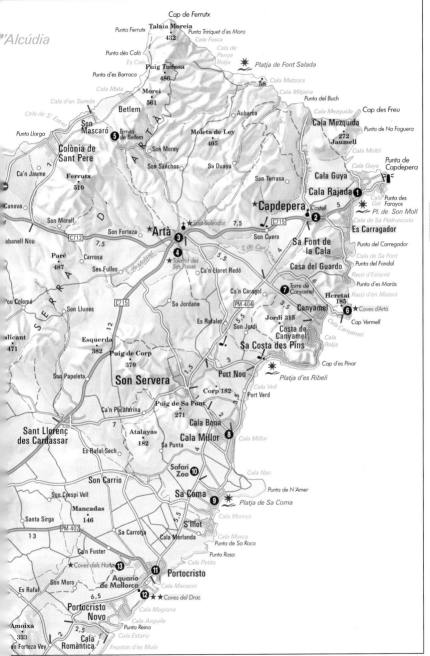

Behind the wall there is a considerable number of foundation and house remains. Archeologists presume that these buildings were used for cult worshiping purposes. In some of them the central pillar, which had supported the ceiling and is known to be a typical feature of this prehistoric civilization's architecture, is still standing.

Ermita de Betlem

North of Artà a small side road leads to the thinly populated and, by Mallorcan standards, lonely Ferrutx Peninsula and **Ermita de Betlem ❺**. This little hermitage is, of all of Mallorca's hermitages, surely the one with the most beautiful location. Unusually, there is no incredible legend of a vision or miracle that is told about this hermitage's origin. In the early 19th century several pious monks withdrew here to the isolation of the Ferrutx Peninsula. As a donation from a large landowner in the region, they received a piece of land upon which stood the ruins of some buildings that had been destroyed by pirates. The monks soon began to rebuild the church, decorating it with pictures and statues. They also established a hostel on this site.

You can climb through the undergrowth of Mallorcan dwarf palms and over creviced rocks to the summit, which is at a height of about 400 meters. Here, well away from the beaten tourist track, you have a magnificent view of the wide Bay of Alcúdia.

ALONG THE COAST

Canyamel and the *Coves d' Artà

From Capdepera the PM-404 runs southwards towards the tiny village of Son Servera. After a few kilometers a

Right: Sa Coma attracts many visitors with its beach of fine sand.

sign indicates the exit, to the left, for the **★Coves d'Artà ❻**, the Caves of Artà. These caves are among the largest on Mallorca and visitors can explore them along a path that leads 500 meters inside. Inside there is a constant temperature of 17°C throughout year. The countless stalactites and stalagtites shimmer in an incredible variety of colors.

To fire the imagination, the grottos have been given names such as "Hall of Hell," "Theater," "Banner Room," "Salon of the Queen," and so on. The largest stalagmite in Europe, which stands 22 meters high, can be found in these caves. With a growth rate of one millimeter per year, however, it will take another 5000 years before it reaches the ceiling, which is another 50 centimeters higher.

From the entrance to the caves you can walk down to the town of Canyamel. If you have a car, you will have to backtrack several kilometers, then turn left, heading in the direction of Canyamel. Shortly before reaching the town, those who are driving will then pass the **Torre de Canyamel ❼**, a 14th-century watchtower with battlements. Especially noteworthy are the large protruding openings from which boiling oil could be poured down upon would-be attackers.

The town of **Canyamel** is a small resort with pretty vacation homes and only a few hotels. Even in the peak season it stays reasonably quiet, and there is scarcely anything to disturb the tranquility of the pine forests and the waves that break gently on the sandy beach – an ideal resort for families with small children, and others who just want to relax.

Cala Millor and Cala Bona

Cala Millor ❽, one of the largest tourist centers on Mallorca's east coast, is the exact opposite of Canyamel. It is as crowded and noisy as Canyamel is empty and quiet, and the rows of hotels are built close together along the broad sandy

The Northeast

beach that is separated from the buildings by a promenade. Cars are not allowed on many of the streets that are lined with pubs, bars, restaurants and discos for every taste.

While Cala Millor, with its fine sand that is especially suitable for children, has been thoroughly taken over by German tourists, in **Cala Bona**, which adjoins it to the north, there are more British vacationers who seem to be less bothered by the stonier, more rugged coast.

Sa Coma and S'Illot

Sa Coma ❾ is a fairly new resort with a beautiful, wide beach of fine sand. The tourists staying in the resort of **S'Illot** used to have it all to themselves, but those times are over. S'Illot has become rather run-down over the years, and Sa Coma has, from a tourist perspective, literally buried its sister resort in the sand. The guests in S'Illot now have to make-do with the narrower, less attractive beach that is directly in front of their hotels.

The beach of fine sand at **Cala Moreya**, on the other hand, is quite nice. Since the accommodations in Sa Coma are even newer and are of a better standard, there is a considerable difference in the prices between the two resorts.

Approximately one kilometer west of Sa Coma is the **Safari Zoo** ❿ (*Reserva Africana*), which is worth a visit and is especially fun for children. With a rented car, the minibus or a miniature train, you can take a ride through "Africa." Ostriches, giraffes, zebras and antelopes can be seen from the road, and monkeys play freely in the grounds. You may stop to look and take photographs for as long as you wish, but you are not permitted to leave your vehicle.

Portocristo and the **Dragon's Caves

Portocristo ⓫ was founded as the fishing port for Manacor towards the end of the 19th century. It lies far inland, and has an ideal natural harbor in a wide, shel-

tered bay. Today you will find, almost exclusively, yachts and motorboats at anchor here. It is the most popular marina on Mallorca's east coast.

At the southern end of town is the aquarium **Aquario de Mallorca**. In 115 seawater pools you can learn about the colorful underwater world of the Mediterranean. Only 150 meters further along the road is Portocristo's real attraction, the ****Coves del Drach** ⓬ (Dragon's Caves), which form the most extensive system of caverns on the Balearic Islands. The name of this underground labyrinth comes from a saga, which says that pirates keep their treasure hidden in the cave, under the watchful eye of a dragon.

There is a lake in the Dragon's Caves that is among the largest underground lakes in the world. It measures 180 meters long, 40 meters wide and nine meters deep.

Above: The Dragon's Caves have a fairy tale atmosphere. Right: Manufacturing artificial pearls at the Majorica factory, in Manacor.

In the early 1920s, the Mallorcan Joan Servera Camps began to open the caves to tourism and installed steps, paths, handrails, lights, and seat sat the lake. After some concerts, which were a private initiative and were hugely successful, it was decided to further exploit the tourist potential of the Dragon's Caves in the future. Since then, every group of visitors can hear a short musical performance. Three pieces are performed, one of them consisting of passages from Handel's *Largo*. The musicians are seated in boats that are wreathed in lights and are silently rowed across the lake. Sophisticated lighting effects enhance the event, adding to the romantic atmosphere.

Just 1.5 kilometers from Portocristo, towards Manacor, you will come to the ***Coves dels Hams** ⓭. In these caves, everything is on a smaller scale than in the nearby Dragon's Caves, which is, above all, reflected in the number of visitors. Here it is possible to walk around 350 meters underground. There is also an underground saltwater lake, the level of which rises and falls with the tides. Here, too, musicians glide across the lake in boats and entertain the public. One special feature of these caves is the stalactites that are covered with barb-like growths. It is because of the shape of these stalactites that the caves were given their name, "Harpoon Caves."

THE INTERIOR

Manacor – The Pearl City

The most important reason for visiting the island's second-largest city is the **Majorica Pearl Factory** where completely artificial pearls are manufactured. Well before you reach **Manacor** ⓮ large billboards advertise this, and once you arrive in town, you will find plenty of signs reliably directing you to the factory. During a visit here, you can watch the production of small pieces of jewelry and then, in a shop across the street, you are free to make your purchases.

*Els Calderes Country Estate and Sant Joan

Just 10 kilometers west of Manacor is **Vilafranca de Bonany** ⓯. On one Saturday in October a Melon Festival, the *Festa d'es Meló*, is celebrated and a "Miss Melon" is chosen. Between Vilafranca and Montuïri, at kilometer marker 37, there is an exit to the old country estate of ***Els Calderes** ⓰, which adopted the additional name of, *La otra Mallorca*, the "other Mallorca," in the interest of promoting tourism. Here you have the chance to study the traditional way of life in the Mallorcan countryside, which is vividly demonstrated in the exhibits.

The estate's main house dates from 1750. By taking a tour, you can visit the reception room, a living room with Mallorcan furniture, the private chapel, the wine cellar, a hunting room and the estate owner's study.

The Northeast

You continue through the large dining room, where the table is set for a banquet, and into the music room, where the lady of the house practiced at the grand piano. The tour then leads upstairs to the bedrooms with furnishings from the 18th and 19th centuries, then outside to the stables and finally to the cafeteria where you can relax with a glass of wine.

Three kilometers further north is the town of **Sant Joan** ⓱, which is renowned for its festivals. One of these, celebrated on the first Sunday in October, is the Festival of Blood Sausages (*Festa d'es Bolifarró*), which is famous across the island.

*Petra

Some 10 kilometers northwest of Manacor, at the foot of a long spreading mountain ridge, lies the quiet little town of ***Petra** ⓲. In a park in the center of town there is a memorial to the Franciscan father and founder of the city of San Francisco, Juníper Serra, who was born in Petra on November 24, 1713.

His ***birth house** and the **museum**, which was built with American assistance, are next to each other, and the house is especially interesting. It is built in the style of the early 18th century and clearly shows how a poor family of farm laborers would have lived in those days. In the museum there are numerous maps, drawings and letters that illustrate the work of this missionary.

*Ermita de Nostra Senyora de Bonanay

On the outskirts of Petra there is an exit from the road leading to Felanitx that leads towards the ***Ermita de Nostra Senyora de Bonany ⓳**, a hermitage that is located on the summit of a 317-meter-high mountain. The view from the shady, tree-covered terrace, where stone tables are just waiting for a picnic, is really wonderful. An avenue leads from the terrace

Above: Living like the lord of the manor at Els Calderes, an 18th-century estate.

to the monastery buildings. In the quite modern church, the altar paintings are of Saint Paul and Saint Anthony. In the center of the altar you can see the Mother of God holding a sweetly smiling Baby Jesus in her arms.

The name *Ermita de Nostra Senyora de Bonany*, "Hermitage of our Dear Lady of the Good Year," refers to the year 1600. There had been a long drought and the farmers had watched their harvests withering in the fields. In their distress they prayed to their Madonna and behold, the heavens were opened and rain soaked the dry earth. As a result, despite the drought, the year 1600 turned out to be a good one after all.

Sineu

Sineu ⓴ is a small town, located in the geographical center of Mallorca, that can look back on a long history. Archeological finds indicate that there was a settlement here during the prehistoric Talayot period. Later, the Romans enlarged the town and made it the center of the region's agricultural development. It is said that Sineu had the first, and therefore the oldest, market on the island. The market here is held on Wednesday and is certainly one of Mallorca's most interesting. Alongside the regular market there is also a livestock market and, as a concession to the tourists who are not absent here, there is also a lively, but expensive trade in antiques.

The highest point in town is crowned by the **Parish Church of Mare de Déu dels Angels**. A wide flight of steps leads up to the main portal, above which the winged Lion of Sineu, bearing a shield, keeps watch. This grim-looking king of the animals is the symbol of Saint Mark, and shows everyone who is the town's patron saint.

Artists and collectors should be sure to visit **S'Estacio**, Sineu's former train station which is now an art center.

ARTÀ

🛏 🚭 **S'Abeurador**, C. Abeurador 21, tel: 971 835 230, fax; 971 829 122; small inn, with secluded courtyard; adjoining restaurant uses organic ingredients.

❌ **Na Creu**, C. 31 de Marzo, tel: 971 836 350; simple Mallorcan food, rustic ambience. **Es Serral**, Apartado de Correos 154, tel: 971 835 336; local country fare.

🏛 **Museu Regional d'Artà**, Mon-Fri 10 am-noon, closed Sat and Sun. **Talayot des Ses Paises**, tel: 619 070 010; Mon-Fri 9:30 am-1 pm and 2:30-5 pm, Sat 9:30 am-1 pm, closed Sun.

CALA MILLOR

ℹ **O.I.T.**, Parc de la Mar 2, tel: 971 585409, fax: 971 585 716, and **O.I.T.**, Passeig Maritim, tel: 971 585 864.

🛏 🚭🚭 **Riu Playa Cala Millor**, Urb. Sa. Màniga, tel/fax: 971 585 212; 250 rooms, near the sea.

❌ **Buffet Can Pistoleta**, on the edge of town, tel: 971 585 449; high standards.

🍸 **Pacha's Pub**, C. Sol Naixent Pacha's; the most popular bar in town.

🦁 **Reserva Africana**, daily 9 am-7 pm; during the winter daily 9 am-5 pm.

CALA RAJADA

ℹ **O.I.T.**, Plaça de los Pins, tel: 971 563 033.

🛏 🚭🚭 **Bella Playa**, Av. Cala de l'Agula 125, tel: 971 563 050, fax: 971 565 252; indoor and outdoor pools, pine grove.

❌ **Ses Rotges**, C. Rafael Blanes 21, tel: 971 563 108; one star (Michelin). **La Casita**, C. des Faralló 6, tel: 971 563 731; very good, great atmosphere. **La Finca**, Av. Juan Carlos I, tel: 971 565 386; good fish & int'l dishes.

🍸 **Physical**, C. Leonora Servera; loudest and most popular disco in town. **Café Noah's**, Av. America 2, on the harbor promenade; best bar in town. **Café 3**, Av. America 4, at the harbor; music bar.

🏛 **Casa March**, tel: 971 563 033; some guided tours.

🎪 **Market Day**: Saturday.

CANYAMEL

❌ **Prozada de la Torre**, next to Torre de Canyamel, tel: 971 841 310; specialty is suckling pig from the spit.

🦁 **Caves of Artà**, tel: 971 841293; April-Sept: daily 10 am-7 pm; Oct-March: daily 10 am-5 pm.

CAPDEPERA

❌ **La Fragua**, C. Es Pla den Cosset, tel: 971 565 050; good food in old village smithy.

🍸 **Bar Gaballins**, Plaça de l'Orient.

🏛 **Fort Capdepera**, tel: 971 818 746; April-Sept: daily 10 am-8 pm; Oct-March: daily 9 am-5 pm. **Museu Regional,** Mon-Fri 10 am-noon, closed Sat and Sun.

ELS CALDERES

🏛 **Country Estate**, daily 10 am-7 pm; winter till 5 pm.

🎪 **Festa d'es Meló** in **Vilafranca**, alt. Sats in Oct.

MANACOR

❌ **La Reserva Rotana**, Cami de S'Avall, at km 3, tel: 971 845 685; superb restaurant, in hotel outside town.

🏛 **Pearl Factory Majorica**, Mon-Fri 9 am-1 pm and 3-5 pm, Sat amd Sun 10 am-1 pm. **Archeological Museum**, Tue-Thu 9 am-1 pm, closed Fri-Mon.

MONTUÏRI

❌ **Puig de Sant Miguel**, Ctra. Palma–Manacor at km 31, tel: 971 646 314; good traditional Mallorcan cuisine. **Es Pati de Montuïri**, Ctra. Montuïri–Sant Joan at km 0.7, tel: 971 646 764; good Mediterranean specialties, in hotel with same name.

PETRA

🛏 🚭 **Ermita de Bonany**, tel: 971 561 101; modest.

❌ **Celler Antic**, C. California; simple restaurant with Mallorcan cuisine. **Es Celler**, C. Hospital 46, tel: 971 561 056; plain fare, but delicious.

🏛 **Birth House of Juníper Serra** and **Museum**, tel: 971 561 149; irregular hours between 9 am and 6 pm.

🏛 **Bodega Miguel Oliver**, C. Font 23; wine heaven.

PORTOCRISTO

ℹ **O.I.T.**, C. Gual 31A, tel: 971 820 931.

🛏 🚭 **Felip**, C. Burdils 41, tel: 971 820 750; central.

🍸 **Dhráa**, Ctra. Portocristo–Cala Millor at km 3.7; open-air disco, Thu-Sun during the summer.

🏛 **Dragon Caves**, tel: 971 820 753; daily 10 am-5 pm, admittance every hour on the hour. **Coves dels Hams**, tel: 971 820 988; daily 10 am-5 pm; summer till 6 pm.

🏛 **Acuario de Mallorca**,daily 10:30 am-5 pm; during the winter 11 am-3 pm.

SINEU

🛏 🚭🚭 **Léon de Sineu**, C. dels Buos 129, tel: 971 520 211, fax: 971 855 058; comfortable country hotel.

❌ **Moli d'en Pau**, Cfra. Santa Margarita 25, tel: 971 855 116; windmill atmosphere with charm. **Celler C'an Font**, Sa Plaça, tel: 971 520 313; typical, most famous basement restaurant in town.

🏛 **Market Day**: Wednesday. **Art Center S'Estació.**

SON SERVERA

🛏 🚭🚭🚭 **Eurotel Golf**, Costa de los Pinos, tel: 971 567 600, fax: 971 567 737; golf courses at the door.

❌ **S'Esra de Pula**, Ctra. Son Servera–Capdepera at km 3, tel: 971 567 940; in a restored windmill, good reputation among gourmets.

THE SOUTHEAST

**CALAS DE MALLORCA
PORTOCOLOM
FELANITX AND SURROUNDINGS
CALA D'OR
CALA FIGUERA
THE SOUTHERN TIP
CAPOCORP VELL**

CALAS DE MALLORCA

The coast south of Portocristo is characterized by an abundance of small *calas* (bays), some of which have tiny sandy beaches. From the wide main road, Portocristo to Santanyí, small access roads branch off every few kilometers and lead down to colonies of vacation homes and hotels at the sea.

Visible from quite a distance, **Calas de Mallorca ❶** is a conglomerate of sprawling hotel complexes that are built on a barren, rocky plateau that falls steeply 20 to 30 meters into the sea. The sandy beaches of the small Cala Domingos and the fjord-like Cala Antena are scarcely adequate for the large number of tourists who, to get to the beach, have to climb down the steps that have been cut into the steep cliffs.

Not far from the exit to Calas de Mallorca you will pass the **Exotic Parque**, a tropical garden that keeps many species of birds in lush green jungle or thorny cactus landscapes. Four times a day there is an entertaining parrot show, and for the younger visitors there is also a play area and a children's zoo with animals that can be petted.

Left: Diving territory – along the rocky coast of Portocolom.

PORTOCOLOM

The attractive fishing village of **Portocolom ❷** is located around a lagoon-shaped bay that forms a perfect natural harbor. Sailing yachts and colorful fishing boats lie side by side at anchor, and many people who are just learning to windsurf take advantage of the quiet sea to make their first attempts.

On the western side of the bay is the old harbor town. On the highest point is the church, while lower down, near the water, are the boat sheds. From here you can get to the Sa Punta Peninsula where a black-and-white striped lighthouse guards the entrance to this natural harbor.

From the southern side of the bay you can cross a ridge of hills and quickly arrive at the fjord-like **Cala Marçal**. Every time you wish to swim in the sea here, you have to do a bit of climbing, and the advantage to this is that only a few tourists, those who want somewhere peaceful, seek out this lonely place. From here you can hike southwards, along the coast, to the less overrun beaches of Cala Brafi, Cala Sa Nau and Cala Mitjana.

FELANITX AND SURROUNDINGS

Just 12 kilometers west of Portocolom, on the other side of the hills that run par-

The Southeast

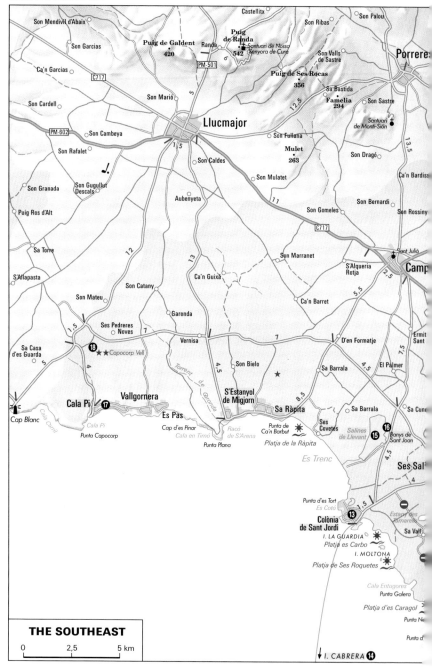

THE SOUTHEAST

0	2,5	5 km

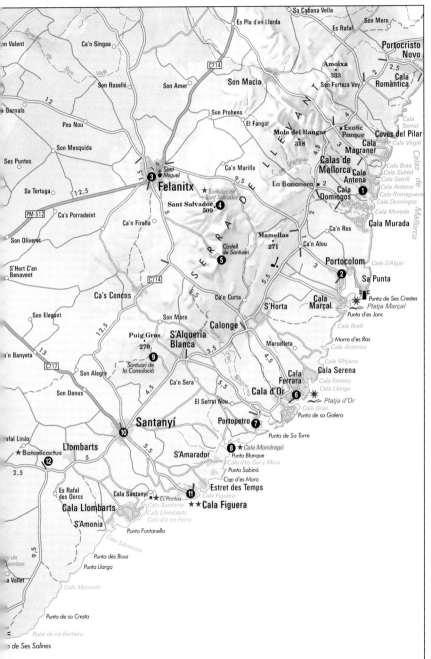

allel to the coast, is the picturesque village of **Felanitx ❸**. The white-painted bases of 25 old windmills that are located on the hills behind the houses give the town a unique profile. As early as Arab times Felanitx was a center, not only for agriculture, but also for the manufacture of ceramic goods. Today, some ceramic works attempt to carry on the old tradition and have set up stalls on the road approaching the village.

The only other interesting sight is the town's **Parish Church of Sant Miquel**, built with gold-colored stone from Santanyí, which stands on the Plaça Font de Santa Margalida. This pretty plaza got its name from its well, which was dug for the public water supply in 1830, the precious source of which – so the locals believe – will never run dry.

A broad flight of steps leads up to the church portal, above which you can see the statute of the village's patron saint

Above: The view from the Santuari de Sant Salvador is magnificent.

and a large rose window. Inside the church, where the colorful glass windows create a magnificent play of light, especially when the sun is shining, there are several noteworthy statues, including, on the left near the front, an unusual representation of Joseph with the Christ Child.

*Santuari de Sant Salvador

Two kilometers beyond the village, on the road from Felanitx to Portocolom, you can take a road to the summit of the Puig de Sant Salvador. The drive up is in itself magnificent, with gnarled olive trees, an old wayside cross, pine woods on steep cliffs, a roadside chapel, tight hairpin curves and then, shortly before the summit, the jaunty projection of a rock with a huge stone cross and the defensive wall of the monastery castle.

On the east side of the garden terrace, on a tower-like substructure, there is a seven-meter-high bronze statue of *Sant Salvador* (the Holy Redeemer), which was donated in 1934 by the canon of the cathedral in Palma, a native of Felanitx. The platform in front of the monument is, doubtless, one of the most thrilling viewing points in all of Mallorca. From a height of 509 meters you can see large parts of the island and, if the air is clear, even the pirate island Cabrera.

Not far from the enormous statue is the **★Santuari de Sant Salvador ❹**, which was built in 1348. This is where pilgrims gather in veneration of a statue of Mary, which, like many of Mallorca's statues of the Madonna, was discovered after the *Reconquista* and was given a place of honor in the monastery.

The artistically worked relief in the entrance hall, depicting the *Last Supper*, is a copy of the decoration on the door of the cathedral in Palma. Beyond the entrance to the restaurant there is a small courtyard and the monastery chapel. The Gothic alabaster altar in the side chapel on the right is of particular interest.

Castell de Santueri

Just two kilometers from the monastery, as the crow flies, lying opposite on a mountain plateau, are the ruins of the **Castell de Santueri ❺**. Although the distance is short, the drive is fairly long because it is not possible to cross the gorge that divides the two mountains. You must return to Felanitx and from there take the C-714, heading south towards Santanyí. A few kilometers outside Felanitx a little mountain road turns to the left, towards the summit. From the parking lot a footpath leads a short distance to the former fortifications, which are actually, more impressive from a distance. All that remains are three defensive towers and part of the outside protective wall.

CALA D'OR

Together, Cala Mitjana, Cala Llonga, Cala d'Or, Cala Gran, Cala Esmeralda, Cala Azul, Cala Ferrera and Cala Serena make up what is known as **Cala d'Or ❻**, a sprawling resort that is a favorite with German tourists in particular. Many of the regular guests call it "Little Ibiza," and it is characterized by low-profile vacation homes, painted snowy white, and hotels and apartment complexes that are set out around the seven bays that reach like fingers into the land. The longest of these "mini fjords," Cala Longa, is the location of the marina, and shops and restaurants have sprung up along the quays. The gourmet temple *Port Petit* can also to be found here. The narrow, rocky bays to the north, Cala d'Or and Cala Gran, end with small sandy beaches, which, unfortunately, are becoming more and more crowded. The remaining bays don't differ significantly from these. They, too, are surrounded by hotels that are built close together. The swell of the waves retreats gently on these sheltered beaches, making them ideal for families with small children.

Portopetro and ★Cala Mondragó

It is foreseeable that **Portopetro ❼** will expand to reach the city limits of Cala d'Or, and that this fishing port – which still retains most of its original character – will also develop into a tourist destination. Fishing boats and yachts still lie in the harbor basin of the sheltered bay, which in earlier times was protected by a watchtower on the Punta de Sa Torre. Street cafés and small restaurants make a pleasant place to linger for a while around the marina.

Not far from Portopetro is one of the most attractive places in this part of the island, **★Cala Mondragó ❽**. The waves recede gently in the sheltered double bay, which is bordered by pine trees, and has two beaches that are joined by a footpath. Only two small hotels were built here before environmentalists ensured that the entire area was placed under legal protection.

The Southeast

Santuari de la Consolació and Santanyí

Four kilometers northeast of Portopetro, shortly before S'Alqueria Blanca, a road branches off to the left and leads to the mountain monastery of **Santuari de la Consolació 9**, which can be seen from far away. From its viewing terrace you can see across the whole southeastern region of Mallorca and to the island of Cabrera.

A few kilometers further on you will come to the little town of **Santanyí 10**. Although it does not have any special features of interest for visitors, a stroll through Santanyí will allow you to experience the authentic atmosphere of a slightly larger Mallorcan community. In the town's narrow streets, the houses of golden yellow sandstone, quarried in the

Above: The Platja des Trenc – Mallorca's last natural beach – is eagerly defended by environmentalists. Right: Stopping for a swim in the idyllic Bay of Cala Pi.

area, are built close together and retain their defensive character. You will come across the **Church of Sant Andreu**, with its beautiful organ, the small **Capilla de Roser** and the **Porta Murada**, which represents the last remains of what were once the town's fortifications.

The market here is held on Wednesdays and is entirely geared towards meeting the needs of the local population. There is no tourist kitsch here.

**CALA FIGUERA

As you drive through the fields, which are filled with almond and carob trees, towards the coast to ****Cala Figuera 11**, at first you won't notice any overwhelming difference between this and many other places on the east coast. If, however, you take the time to make the descent to the end of the bay, you will rub your eyes and wonder if you are still on the tourist island of Mallorca. The lower part of Cala Figuera is, in fact, an extremely picturesque fishing village that, even today, de-

serves the attribute "sleepy." A narrow bay penetrates deep into the land, then divides into two fingers, making the harbor resemble the letter "Y."

If you take a walk around the harbor you will soon find that you are walking on wooden planks – secured to the cliff – that are directly over the water. Because the cliffs rise so steeply it was not possible to build a path, and many of the boat sheds are hewn right out of the cliffs. Figuera is unrivalled as the fishing harbor with the most atmosphere in all Mallorca.

THE SOUTHERN TIP

Ses Salines

The road to **Cap de Ses Salines**, Mallorca's southernmost point, leads through the private property of the March family. It is bordered on both sides by barbed wire and ends at a gate in front of a lighthouse. From here there is a footpath that leads to the **Platja d'es Caragol**, about one kilometer away.

The region around **Ses Salines**, barren, lacking water and withered by dry winds, presented itself as the ideal location for a unique botanical garden, the **★Botanicactus ⑫**. On 12 hectares of land visitors will find every imaginable variety of cacti, all arranged in a very pleasing and attractive manner. Typical Mallorcan plants can also be seen, and there are various tropical biotopes, desert plants, an old water-wheel from Arabian times, a windmill, artificial fish ponds, palm groves and shady tree-lined avenues.

Colònia de Sant Jordi

The fishing port of **Colònia de Sant Jordi ⑬**, which may initially make a somewhat boring impression, is located on a rocky plateau from which mounds of weathered rock break off and fall into the sea. The pretty harbor is surrounded by small restaurants and cafés, and excursion boats depart from here to the island of **Cabrera ⑭**, which has been declared a nature conservation area.

Right behind the modern hotel colony on the northern edge of the town, begins **Platja des Trenc**, Mallorca's last large natural beach, as yet unspoiled by development. The beach is five kilometers long and is divided in the middle by a rocky terrace upon which Ses Covetes, an unattractive complex of vacation homes, is located.

Located directly behind the new hotels of Colónia de Sant Jordi are the pink-colored lagoons of the salt pools, the **Salines de Llevant ⓭**, which stretch far inland and have been used for obtaining salt since Phoenician times. Using a process that has not changed much since 600 B.C., seawater is brought via canals to shallow ponds, where it evaporates, leaving behind layers of salt-containing minerals.

At the edges of the salt pools anyone who is interested in biology can observe numerous rare, salt-resistant plants. The salt works attract more than 150 species of birds, including flamingos, sandpipers, ducks, ospreys, avocets and many more.

Six kilometers north of Colónia de Sant Jordi, on the road to Palma, are the **Banys de Sant Joan ⓰** (Baths of Saint John), the only thermal springs on the island. Even the Romans appreciated their healing powers and soaked their rheumatic and arthritic joints in the water, which has a constant temperature of 38°C.

Cala Pi

A short detour off the coast road, which runs a little inland, to the villa resort of **Cala Pi ⓱** is well worthwhile. The vacation villas are widely spread out on a plateau, high above the sea, and the central hotel complex blends into the landscape. A rocky spur, occupied by a lonely old watchtower, juts out into the sea allowing you to can gaze out at an unspoiled view of the coast that drops off sharply, like a steep stairway, into the sea.

At the eastern end of the resort the cliff face drops vertically down to a small bay, ending at a sandy beach. A steep, signed flight of steps leads down from the hotel complex to the sea. The narrow bay, which penetrates far inland, is popular with sailors who regularly use it as a place to anchor their yachts.

From the path high above the sea, which leads to the headland at Cap Blanc, there are wonderful views of the sea, which has an intense deep blue color. No one takes much notice, therefore, of the fact that the land around the lighthouse, which can be seen from far and wide, is closed to the public.

**CAPOCORP VELL

On the southern coast road, situated among small picturesque farmhouses, close to the exit to Cala Pi, are the prehistoric ruins of the Talayot settlement of **Capocorp Vell ⓲**, which are still relatively well preserved and are second in importance after those at Artà.

The older, round towers were presumably the center of a settlement that was later surrounded by a protective circular wall. The square towers were apparently not added to the defensive complex until a later date. They are better preserved and archeologists believe that they date from the 6th century B.C. One of the existing towers still stands approximately six meters high.

The lower, windowless room in the tower can be entered by a narrow passage. However, although the researchers who began to dig here in 1919 found a human skeleton, it is not thought that this was a burial chamber. A pillar supports the intermediate ceiling that is made of stone slabs. The next story was covered by a flat roof that was still been in existence at the beginning of the 20th century.

Outside the walls are the remains and foundations of other buildings that were connected by passageways.

CALA FIGUERA

Cala Figuera, C. S. Pedro 28, tel: 971 645 251, fax: 971 645 252; beautifully located on the steep coast. **Hostal Playa**, on the east side of Cala Santanyí, tel: 971 645 409, fax: 971 645 397; has a beach with beach bar.

Sa Pizzeria, C. La Marina 11; shrill atmosphere in a 60-year-old former chapel, also has tables outside.

CALAS DE MALLORCA

Exotic Parque, tel/fax: 971 183 492; daily 10 am-7 pm, in the winter until 5 pm. **La Bananera**, daily 10 am-5 pm.

CALA D'OR

O.I.T., Av. Cala Llonga, tel/fax: 971 657 463.

Riu Cala Esmeralda, Urb. Cala Esmeralda 37, tel: 971 657 111, fax: 971 657 156; 150 rooms and 2 pools (1 fresh, 1 seawater). **Tamarix**, Av. Cala d'Or, tel: 971 657 851, fax: 971 659 009; good value for money.

Hostal D'Neptuno, Av. Boulevard d'Or 19, tel: 971 657 084, fax: 971 658 219.

Port Petit, Av. Cala Llonga, tel: 971 643 039; "little harbor" for big gourmets, the best restaurant in town. **Bona Taula**, 4 km before Cala d'Or in Calonge, C. Rafael Adrover 3, tel: 971 167 147; first-class meat dishes from the grill. **La Cascina**, in Calonge, C. Cala Llonga 22, tel: 971 167 152; one of the island's best Italian restaurants. **Es Clos**, 9 km before Cala d'O in S'Alqueria Blanca, C. Convento 17, tel: 971 653 404; very good food and fine wines in a finca with local atmosphere.

Chic Palace, in town center, area's most popular disco. **Manni's Bar**, in town center, German draft beer, very popular with the many Germans who regularly vacation in Mallorca. **Bar Telefono**, in Calonge, C. de Rafael Adrover 3; only open on weekends, live music, is not generally overrun by tourists.

CALA PI

San Miguel, near the old watchtower on the hills above town, best restaurant of the town.

CAPOCORP VELL

Prehistoric Settlement, Fri-Wed 10 am-5 pm, closed Thu.

COLÒNIA DE SANT JORDI

O.I.T., C. Doctor Barraquer 5, tel: 971 656 073.

Don Leon, C. Sol, tel: 971 655 561, fax: 971 655 566; private rocky beach, not far to sandy beach. **Cabo Blanco**, C. Carabela 2, tel: 971 655 075, fax: 971 656 318; directly on the sea.

Ibiza, C. Esmeralda Solar 25, tel: 971 655 552, fax: 971 649 501; 16 residential units, each unit sleeps 4.

Marisol, at the harbor, C. Gabriel Roca 63, tel: 971 655 070; one of the best harbor restaurants. **Port Blau**, on the harbor promenade, tel: 971 656 555; unbeatable fish menu.

Banys de Sant Joan, daily 9-11 am, small hotel.

Boat tours to **Cabrera**, tel: 971 649 034.

FELANITX

Vista Hermosa, Ctra. a Portocolom km 6, tel: 971 824 960; idyllic park, expensive cuisine, first-class hotel

Castell de Santueri, mid-May-Sept: 9 am to dusk.

Ceramics: Céramicas Mallorca, C. S. Agusti 50-58.

PORTOCOLOM

O.I.T., Ronda del Creuer Balears, tel: 971 825 768.

Caesar, C. Llaud 8, tel: 971 825 302, fax: 971 824 696; quiet location, many regular German guests. **Celler Sa Sinia**, at the harbor, C. Pescadores 25, tel: 971 824 323; very good fish restaurant, fish and lobster specialties.

PORTOPETRO

Club Cala Barca, Urb. Sa Barca Trancada, tel: 971 658 247, fax: 971 658 023; three-story apartment houses with well-maintained grounds, four pools.

Maritimo, **Ca'n Martina**, **Celler Ca'n Xina** and **Portopetro**, four equally good restaurants around the harbor.

SANTANYÍ

Es Moli, C. Consolació 19, tel: 971 653 358; outstanding Mediterranean cuisine, shady inner-courtyard of an old mill. **Vienna**, in the hamlet Cas Concos, C. Metge Olbvador 13, tel: 971 842 026; restaurant with very lively bistro atmosphere, the house specialty is *Wiener Schnitzel* with a superb Mediterranean touch.

Market Day: Wednesday.

SA RÀPITA

Ca'n Pep, Av. Miramar 16, tel: 971 640 102; excellent fish restaurant. **Club Náutico,** directly at the marina. **Brisas**, Av. Miramar 23, near the marina, tel: 971 640 842; good value for money.

SES SALINES

Casa Manolo, in the bodega Barahona, Plaça San Bartolomé 2, tel: 971 649 130; original bar. **Es Pinaret,** Ctra. Ses Salines–C. de Sant Jordi at km 2.5, tel: 971 649 230; excellent food at reasonable prices.

Botanicactus, just outside town on the PM-610 towards Santanyí, tel: 971 649 494; daily 9 am-7 pm.

The Southeast

81

EAST OF PALMA

S'ARENAL
TOWARDS ALGAIDA
PUIG DE RANDA
LLUCMAJOR

S'ARENAL

At the eastern end of the wide Bay of Palma are the towns of **Can Pastilla, Platja de Palma** (**Las Maravillas**) and **S'Arenal ❶**. The first was once a small fishing port, both of the others consisted of nothing more than a beach, an isolated monastery and pine forests. Today, all three combine to form one large built-up area, with a total of 50,000 hotel beds, that stretches for kilometers along the flat sandy beach. This was the seed for the island's tourist boom – this is where the foundations were laid for Mallorca's rise to become the most popular tourist destination in Europe.

In the Bay of Palma there is only one mode – vacation pure. Here you will find six palm-tree-lined kilometers of sea promenade, covered with white sand, colorful parasols, chaise lounges holding sparsely-clad people, splashing waves, happily contented children playing in the water, and almost always bright sunshine, blue sea and blue sky.

Now a word about Mallorca's "German phenomenon": the times are long past in which primitive wooden stands advertised typical German food with

Left: Glass blowing is literally hot work – a glass blower near Algaida.

badly spelled signs. Today you will find tourist menus in perfect German.

At the beach, a team of blue-haired men in costumes with red-white-and-blue diamond patterns strides and jumps around between the chaise lounges and urges tourists to try the specialty "white sausages" in the *Hofbräuhaus*. On the promenade, Mickey Mouse and Donald Duck distribute flyers that are meant to guide guests to the right restaurant. The choices are inexhaustible, and there are countless restaurants with names like *Oberbayern, Bierkönig, Schinkenbude, Carussel, Bamboleo* and *Ballermann, Ballermann, Ballermann.*

The latter, a much-beloved name, was apparently coined by German tongues that had been made weary by alcohol and tried to pronounce the Spanish word *balneario* (swimming place, a section of beach with a beach bar). *Ballermann* was simply easier for them to say.

And the rumors are indeed true. Particularly in the evening, beer, sangría and vodka flow, sometimes to an excess that is not at all to the liking of the local inhabitants. Since television reports in recent years have repeatedly shown pictures of loud drunken German tourists, and beamed them across the world, the planners in the island's local tourist offices began to fear that Mallorca's image

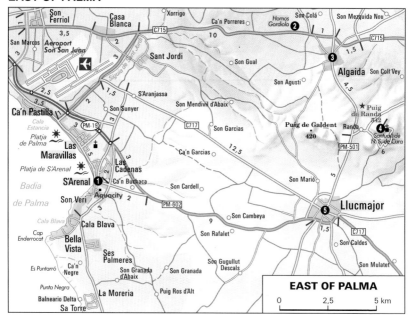

EAST OF PALMA

0   2,5   5 km

would be seriously damaged. As a result, all filming at *Ballermann* is forbidden. Sangría, which was once jointly consumed by groups, from plastic buckets, with meter-long straws, may now only be served in glasses, and even the *Ballermann* sign has been removed from the "Balneario 6" section of the beach.

Whoever has the impression that alcohol and vice predominate in S'Arenal is, however, under a misconception. During the day there is plenty on offer in addition to the beach: bus trips, cheap rental cars and sightseeing in Palma.

At the southern end of S'Arenal there is a water fun park, **Aquacity**, a paradise for water rats, with huge waves, thrilling adventure pools, raging white water that can be ridden on a large inner tube, and slides of gigantic proportions

If you are looking for tranquility – and even this can be found in S'Arenal – you

Right: Tourists visiting Mallorca may no longer slurp their Sangría from a bucket, but they still use meter-long straws.

need only make your way between Balnearios 5 and 6, preferably via the Padre Bartholomé Salva, and head three blocks away from the sea. Behind the Riu Bali Hotel, on a wooded hill, you will find a **Franciscan Monastery** with an interesting modern church.

TOWARDS ALGAIDA

From Palma, the C-715 leads in a straight line westwards through the center of the island, via Algaida and Montuïri, to Mallorca's second-largest city, Manacor.

Shortly before you reach Algaida, on the left, are the **Glass-Blowing Works La Gordiola ❷**, which are located in a fortress-like building. On the lower floor you can watch the glass blowers at their strenuous work and in a salesroom you can purchase their beautifully crafted products. On the upper floor there is a small museum, the **Museu de Vidre**, which has exhibits of antique glass and information about the tradition of glass making. La Gordiola, the island's oldest

glass-blowing works, was founded in 1719.

A good reason for a stop in **Algaida ❸**, following your visit, is to eat in one of the fine restaurants, for which it is famous.

★PUIG DE RANDA

The PM-501 now leads through very attractive landscapes, southwards from Algaida, to the small town of **Randa**, and then on to the ★**Puig de Randa ❹**, which rises suddenly out of the plain to a height of 542 meters, like a large stone block that is almost completely level on top. By means of many tight hairpin curves, the road snakes up the mountainside, on which three monasteries of equal significance are located.

The monastery of **Santuari de Nostra Senyora de Gràcia** is the first one you come to. The abbey was founded by the Franciscan Pater Antonio Caldés in 1440. The buildings seem to cling to the steep cliffs. This pious monk had sought a retreat in a cave in the loneliness of the

mountain, in order to devote himself to intensive prayer and nearness to the Lord. A chapel was built as early as 1497, and it was altered and enlarged in the 18th century. A high, overhanging rock seems to protect the monastery like a vaulted roof. There is a terrace with magnificent views across the central plain and to the sea of houses that is Llucmajor. In the distance you can see Palma and the island's southern coast, and in clear weather you can even see the island of Cabrera.

Just a little higher is the hermitage of **Ermita de Sant Honorat**, which is a good half-century older. In 1395, the owners of the surrounding lands donated this place to the pious hermit Arnaldo Desbrull, so he could henceforth give testimony to his faith.

On the summit of the Puig de Randa, behind the antennae of a radio transmitter, is Mallorca's oldest abbey, **Santuari de Nostra Senyora de Cura**. This large monastic complex is inseparably connected with Ramón Llull (1235-1316), one of Mallorca's greatest sons

and one of Europe's most important clergymen.

Raimundus Llullus, as the Latin version of his name reads, was born in Palma, probably in 1235, just a short time after the *Reconquista*. The son of a noble family, he grew up at the royal court. Although he was legally married and the father of two children, he could not stop chasing other women and was untiring in his pursuit of the ladies at court. At the age of 30 he fell in love with a married woman, Ambrosia de Castellano. On one occasion, when he was riding on horseback, following his beloved into church, Ambrosia ripped open her blouse and showed him her breasts, which were terribly deformed by illness. Ramón, in shock, renounced worldly pleasures and withdrew to a cave on the Puig de Randa to repent for his wasted life. There he

Above: From the terrace of the Santuari de Nostra Senyora de Cura you can see Palma and the peaks of the Tramuntana.

founded a school for priests and missionaries and devoted himself to philosophical and theological matters. He wrote many of his works in Catalan, and thus paved the way for this regional idiom to become a literary language.

Today, the monastery is one of the most important places of pilgrimage in Mallorca. In the courtyard, surrounded by arcades, which because of its size appears cold and stark, there is accommodation for pilgrims. In a small park on the right-hand side is a monument to Ramón Llull. Numerous painted tiles illustrating the life of Mary adorn the arcade behind the park. Also there is the entrance to the plain but elegant church in which pilgrims come to plead before *Nostra Senyora de Cura*, a statue of Mary, to be healed from illness.

Paintings on glass, which are on display in the monastery, illustrate the turbulent life of Ramón Llull, and the library exhibits books and manuscripts from the 16th and 17th centuries. In the abbey's former refectory, there is a simple restaurant with a terrace that offers a panoramic view, from Palma to the Tramuntana. In clear weather conditions you can even make out the mighty block of rock upon which the castle of Alaró stands. To the right, behind the castle, you can see the Puig Major, and further to the right is the city of Inca, with the long drawn-out Puig de Inca.

LLUCMAJOR

Below the mountain Randa is **Llucmajor ❺**, which plays a significant role in southern Mallorca, once as an industrial center and today as a market town. It has few attractions to offer visitors and the inhabitants are largely spared the influence of tourism. The town received its name from the Romans who called this region *Lucus Major* (large wood).

On October 25, 1349, an event that was to prove of great significance for Mallorca took place just outside the city gates. James III, who had already been defeated twice by his Aragonese opponent Pere IV, had landed on the east coast. Once again he would attempt to regain Mallorca for his crown. He advanced towards Palma with his army, which was weakened by illness. The much stronger troops of his enemy were marching to meet him. The two sides met at the gates of Llucmajor and James lost this, his last battle, when he was beheaded by an enemy soldier. At the western approach to town you can see a **stone cross** that marks this cruel event. In Llucmajor itself there is a monument that shows the dying king. The unfortunate ruler was laid to rest in the town's parish church of Sant Miguel. Later his remains were transferred to Palma where they were interred in the cathedral, beside those of James II.

Around the Plaça Espanya, which is near the **Monument to the Shoemakers**, there is a bustling vegetable market that is held every Wednesday, Friday and Sunday morning.

ALGAIDA

☒ **Hostal S'Algaida**, Ctra. Palma–Manacor at km 21, tel: 971 665 109; the best address in town.

Es 4 Vents, Ctra. Palma–Manacor at km 21.7, tel: 971 665 173; superb food from the grill.

Ca'n Mateu, Ctra. Vieja de Manacor at km 21.7, tel: 971 665 036.

🏛 **Museu de Vidre** (**La Gordiola Glass-Blowing Works**), Mon-Sat 9 am-8 pm, Sun 9 am-1 pm.

S'ARENAL AND PLATJA DE PALMA

ℹ **O.I.T.**, Plaça Reina M. Cristina, tel: 971 440 414.

🛏 ❸❸❸ **Sporthotel Delta**, 6 km south of S'Arenal, tel/fax: 971 741 000; everything for a sporting vacation: swimming, tennis and bicycle rental.

❸ **Youth Hostel**, Alberg de Juventud, C. Costa Brava 13, tel: 971 260 892; reservations tel: 902 111 188; open all year, reservations are essential.

☒ **Sa Farinera**, C. Son Fangos 7, tel: 971 262 011; mainly meat dishes, in an old windmill. **Ca's Cotxer**, Ctra. de Arenal 31, tel: 971 262 049; Mallorcan contrast program.

🍸 The following establishments are between Balnearios 5 and 8, either on the beach promenade, in the parallel street behind it, or in the side streets; all of the discos and pubs are within a few meters of each other: **Bambolea**, **Bierkönig**, **Bolero**, **Cabo Blanco**, **Carussel**, **Goldene Mitte**, **Hofbräuhaus Latino**, **Joy Palace**, **Oberbayern**, **Paradies**, **Regine's**, **RIU**, **Palace**, **Royal Suite** and **Schinkenbude Zorbas**.

🏛 **Monastery San Francisco**, Mon-Sat 9:30 am-1 pm and 4-6 pm, Sun 9:30 am-1 pm.

🚜 **Market Day**: Thursday.

🏊 **Aquacity**, tel: 971 440 000; daily 10 am-6 pm.

RANDA

🛏 ❸❸ **Es Recó de Aanda**, C. Sa Font 13, tel: 971 660 997, fax: 971 662 558; in a 17th-century country house, away from beach and disco crowd, pool.

❸ **Santuari de Cura**, on the Puig de Ronda, tel: 971 120 260; simple monastery rooms (*Hospederia*), with a fantastic view.

☒ **Es Recó de Ronda**, restaurant in the hotel of the same name; very good Mallorcan cuisine, excellent lamb and fish dishes, e.g., perch with wild fennel. **Celler de Ronda**, C. Església 20, tel: 971 660 969; simple, but cheaper than Es Recó de Ronda.

LLUCMAJOR

☒ **Moli**, at the southern end of town; restaurant in a restored windmill. **Cafe Colòn**, Plaça d'Espanya 17, tel: 971 660 002; café, popular with everyone.

🚜 **Market**: Wed, Fri and Sun 8:30 am-2 pm.

Map p. 84

METRIC CONVERSION

Metric Unit	US Equivalent
Meter (m)	39.37 in.
Kilometer (km)	0.6241 mi.
Square Meter (sq m)	10.76 sq. ft.
Hectare (ha)	2.471 acres
Square Kilometer (sq km)	0.386 sq. mi.
Kilogram (kg)	2.2 lbs.
Liter (l)	1.05 qt.

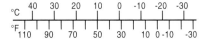

TRAVEL PREPARATIONS

Entering the Country

Citizens of the EU (European Union) who wish to visit Mallorca for tourist purposes require only an identity card or passport, which must be valid for at least three months. US citizens with ordinary passports, valid for a minimum of six months, who wish to visit Spain as tourists for up to 90 days, do not require a visa.

A valid identity card or passport is also required when checking into a hotel or renting a car.

Traveling to Mallorca by Air

If you are flying to Mallorca from the US, chances are you will have to change planes somewhere in Europe.

If you are flying to Mallorca directly from Europe, there are a variety of possibilities. There are both charter and scheduled flights from all of the major European airports, and even some of the smaller ones, often with several flights per day. These international flights land at the island's new airport, Sant Joan, which is just 10 kilometers east of Palma. Flights and "last minute" vacation packages are often available from a number of European airports at bargain prices, with flights, for example, starting at around US $100.

Traveling to Mallorca by Ship

There is a daily ferry service from Barcelona to Palma. The crossing takes about eight hours. The more expensive high-speed ferry takes about half as long, however, it is only in service during the peak tourist season. For additional information contact *Trasmediterránea Palma*, tel: 902 454 645. Prices for the crossing start at about US $40 per person, and about $75 for a car.

Exchanging Money

The Spanish currency is the peseta (pta). Bills come in 10,000, 5000, 2000 and 1000 pta denominations. Coins are valued at 500, 200, 100, 50, 25, 10, 5 and 1 pta. The 500 and 100 pta coins, which are very similar in both size and color, can easily be confused. There are two different versions of the 25 pta coins, one is large and silver, the other is small, bronze and has a hole in the middle. The 5 pta coins are almost always referred to as *duros*, and the new 1 and 5 pta coins are very small!

For US $1 you will receive approximately 170 ptas. The best way to change money is by using the multi-currency cash machines at the banks (*telebanco*), which also accept EC cards. The largest amount you can withdraw at one time is 30,000 ptas, about US $175. If you prefer travelers' checks to cash, they can be cashed at currency exchange offices and banks, often at better rates than cash. Horrendous fees are often charged for Eurocheques and in many cases they are not accepted at all. Credit cards, on the other hand, are widely used and are accepted by most hotels, in many shops, gas stations and restaurants. Banks and credit unions are only open in the morning.

Spanish Tourist Offices Abroad

UNITED KINGDOM: 23-23 Manchester Square, London, W1M 5AP, tel: 020 7486 8077, fax: 020 7486 8034. *UNITED STATES OF AMERICA:* 666 5th Avenue,

35th Floor, New York, NY 10103, tel: (212) 265-8822, fax: (212) 265-8864.

Diplomatic Representation on Mallorca
IRELAND: C. San Miguel, Palma, tel: 971 719 244. *UK:* Plaça Mayor 3D, Palma, tel: 971 712 445. *USA:* Avd. Jaume III 26, Palma, tel: 971 722 660.

Spanish Embassies and Consulates
IRELAND: 17A Merlyn Park, Ballsbridge, Dublin 4, tel: 01-269-1640. *UK:* 39 Chesham Place, London SW1X 8SB, tel: 0171-235-5555, fax: 0171-259-5392. *USA:* Embassy, 2375 Pennsylvania Ave. NW, Washington, DC 20037, tel: (202) 452-0100, fax: (202) 833-5670. Consulate, 150 East 58th Street, 30th Floor, New York, NY 10155, tel: (212) 355-4080, fax: (212) 644-3751.

Climate and Best Time to Travel
Many Central and Northern Europeans spend the winter on the sunshine island Mallorca where the temperature rarely falls below 12°C. The high humidity, however, makes this kind of temperature feel much colder. So, if you are visiting during the winter, it is important to make sure that heating is available in your accommodation. There can be snow in the Tramuntana Mountain Range in January and February.

In the winter you can expect rain in all parts of the island, however, compared to Central or Northern European levels, the amount of precipitation is generally moderate. Around Christmas warm southern winds often create a weather phenomenon that the locals call "little summer."

The best time for a sporting vacation is April: temperatures are spring-like, but not yet hot, so walking or cycling tours aren't too strenuous. From mid-May onwards temperatures climb and the number of rainy days declines rapidly. This marks the beginning of the swimming season. From mid-June to September temperatures are usually around 30°C and can be considerably higher. Water temperatures during the summer reach between 25° and 28°C. Along the coast a steady breeze ensures that the heat is not too intense.

The fall is also a very pleasant time to visit Mallorca. Many plants bloom again in a second, short season, the sea isn't much cooler than in summer, and there are fewer tourists than in the peak season.

Clothing and Equipment
During the summer months you should pack a light rain jacket and thin sweater, as well as a hat, sunglasses and sunscreen. During the winter a water- and windproof jacket and a warm sweater are essential.

If you wear your beach clothes into town don't be surprised if you provoke derogatory remarks from the locals. If you visit a restaurant in beach clothing you will generally find that you won't be served. Formal clothing – especially when going out – is considered important by the Spanish. For men, the minimum requirement is a sports jacket and a well-pressed pair of trousers. For women, a dress or skirt. For most of your stay, however, more casual clothing – jeans, sports shirts or casual blouses and sandals – will be sufficient.

TRAVELING ON MALLORCA

Transportation
Bus: Mallorca has an excellent network of buses that offers many good connections; Palma is the hub. Beach resorts near the capital have especially frequent services, but it may be more difficult to find a connection between two smaller towns. Bus schedules are available in hotels or can be obtained from local tourist offices and the island's central information office in Palma, which are listed in the Info section at the end of each chapter. In the summer months, due to heavy traf-

fic, be prepared for considerable delays and over crowding. Palma's central bus station is at Plaça Espanya.

Train: Palma's train station is also located at Plaça Espanya. There are two railway lines. The historical train, named "Red Lightning," runs several times a day between Palma and Sóller. From Sóller you can travel on to Port de Sóller with a picturesque old-fashioned streetcar. The trip to Sóller, through the Tramuntana Mountains, across several bridges and through 13 tunnels, is fascinating. The train even stops so you can take photographs. For tickets call tel: 971 752 051.

The second railway line runs from Palma to Inca, several times daily. For tickets and information, tel: 971 752 245.

Taxi: Charges for taxis are comparable to those of Central Europe. Within Palma taxi drivers charge according to the taximeter; in all of the island's other towns, prices are displayed at the taxi stands. The following are contact phone numbers for local taxi services:

Taxi Services Palma de Mallorca: 971 755 440; 971 298 200; 971 401 414.
Taxi Services Andratx: 971 671 664.
Taxi Services Caviá: 971 680 970.

Rental Cars: There are over 20,000 rental cars on Mallorca, and this is really the best means of transportation. It is usually cheaper to rent locally than to reserve a car from home before coming. All of the car rental firms have representatives at the airport in Palma and near large hotels. The cars do vary considerably, not only in price, but also in age and quality. A small car for instance, can cost approximately US$30 per day, including unlimited kilometers and comprehensive insurance without deductible. You don't have to have an international driver's license; a national driver's license is sufficient. A green insurance card is advisable. Payment is generally required in advance, but they do not usually require a deposit.

The maximum speed limit in developed areas is 50 kilometers per hour, on country roads 90, and on the highways 120 kilometers per hour. Unleaded fuel is available everywhere. Seatbelts must be worn by everyone in the car!

When you park on the street, in spaces that are marked with a blue line, you must obtain a parking ticket from a nearby machine, and leave this, clearly visible, in the car. Yellow lines mark areas where parking is absolutely forbidden. It is essential to avoid parking in such areas, or overstaying the limit of the time allowed. An army of policewomen – called *oreros* (gold-makers) by the local population – swarms across the island issuing parking tickets and immobilizing, or having towed, vehicles that are illegally parked.

A useful hint: if a parking ticket is paid at the relevant police station within 24 hours, many local authorities will reduce the fine by 50 percent.

Motor Scooters: If you only need to be mobile within the area near where you are staying, a motor scooter is also a good way to get around. Rental offices can be found all over the island.

Bicycles: Even though many charter airlines only make a small charge, or none at all, for transporting bicycles (between $15 and $25), an arrangement of this kind is only essential for passionate cyclists. Bicycle rental firms, which offer all kinds of bicycles at very reasonable prices, are located across the island. The *Sporthotel Delta*, in Cala Blava (tel/fax: 971 741 000), specializes in cycling trips. Note: cycling on the island's often narrow roads can be quite dangerous.

Boats: Some places can be reached by boat; the island of Dragonera, for example, from Sant Elm; Cala Tuent and the beach of Sa Calobra from Port de Sóller; the island of Cabrera from Colònia de Sant Jordi; and the *Hotel Formentor* from Port de Pollença or Port d'Alcúdia. From Port d'Alcúdia there is also a ferry to Menorca. From Magaluf you can have the unusual experience of a 2-hour submarine trip with *Nemo Submarines*.

PRACTICAL TIPS FROM A TO Z

Accommodation

The symbols used in the Info sections at the end of each chapter have the following meanings: ☺☺☺ = Luxury: a double room (with double occupancy) from 16,000 ptas. ☺☺ = Moderate: from 8000 to 16,000 ptas. ☺ = Budget: less than 8000 ptas.

Hotels: From the three-star category upwards you can be sure of having air conditioning and satellite TV. However, there are considerable price differences within the same category, i.e., larger hotels in the main tourist resorts are cheaper than those in the island's interior or the Tramuntana Mountains.

The hotel association *Reis de Mallorca* offers numerous, select traditional hotels between one and five stars. Reservations through *Reis de Mallorca*, C. Thomás Forteza 55A, Palma de Mallorca, Spain, tel: 971 770737, fax: 971 464013.

Vacation Apartments and Houses: Like hotels, they can be booked through the usual travel agents, but it is cheaper to rent these once you are in Mallorca. Look for ads in *Mallorca Magazine*.

Fincas and Rural Tourism: If you would prefer to stay in style in a finca, you will also find offers from travel agents. In contrast to Central or Northern Europe, rural vacations are by no means in the lower price range. Their exclusiveness, style and comfort have a certain price. The owners of the hotel fincas, which are often quite luxurious, have joined together to form an association that sets standards and advertises centrally (also see the section on Rural Tourism, page 93).

Monastery Accommodation: This can sometimes be the cheaper alternative. The following monasteries offer basic accommodation for tourists: Lluc Monastery (70 rooms, some with bathrooms); Ermita de Sant Salvador, near Felanitx; Cura Monastery on the Randa, near Lluc-major; the monastery on the Puig de María near Pollença; the Bonany Monastery at Petra; and the Monte-Sión Monastery at Porreres.

Mountain Hostels: Currently, the only one is the *Refugi Tossals Verds*; meals are also available. It is located in the Tramuntana, in the Maçanlella region (directions: via Lloseta to the Finca Almedra, then 45 min. on foot), tel: 971 182 027.

Electricity

The standard voltage in all hotels is 220 volts. In many older houses the voltage is still 110 volts. This affects tourists less than it does the "new-Mallorcan" homeowners. You will, however, need a plug adaptor for electrical appliances.

Emergencies

The central emergency telephone number (multilingual operators) for the police, fire department and ambulance is 112. You can also use the following numbers across the island: National Police (*Policia Nacional*): 091; City Police (*Policia Local*): 092; *Guárdia Civil*: 062; fire department – Palma: 080; fire department – outside Palma: 085; ambulance: 061; lifeboat: 971 900 202; R.A.C.E. (auto club): 971 737 346.

Festivals

January 5: Procession of the Magi, in Palma. *January 17:* Festival of Saint Anthony, procession of animals that have been blessed, in Palma. *January 19:* Palma celebrates its patron, Saint Sebastian, with a procession and street festivals. *February:* Colorful Carnival processions across the island. *March/April:* During Holy Week (*Semana Santa*) there are pilgrimages and processions across the island. *Fourth Sunday in Lent:* Festival of Bread and Fish (*Festa d'es Pài es Pex*) across the island. *May 11:* Celebration of the victory over the pirates (*Moros i Cristians*) in Sóller. *July 16:* Boat processions honoring the Protectress of the

Fishermen (*Virgen del Carmen*), in all of the harbor towns. *First Sunday in September:* Procession of the Holy Beata (*Festa de la Beata*), with floats, local inhabitants wear traditional dress, in Santa Margalida. *Fourth Sunday in September:* Wine Festival, with wine tasting, in Binissalem. *First Sunday in October:* Festival of the Blood Sausage (*Festa di Botifaró*), parade and tasting of local sausage products. *Varying Sundays in October:* Melon Festival (*Festa d'es Meló*), in Vilafranca de Bonany. *October 20/21:* The Night of the Virgins (*Nit de ses Verges*), young men sing at the windows of their beloved and flirt their way through the night. *Second Thursday in November:* Good Thursday (*Dijous Bo*), harvest celebration and agricultural fair, in Inca. *December 31:* Flag Festival (*Festa de l'Estandard*), commemorating James I's conquest of the city on December 31, 1229, in Palma.

National Holidays

January 1: New Year's Day (*Año nuevo*).
January 6: Epiphany (*Los Reyes Magos*).
Holy Week: Thursday and Good Friday (*Juevos Santo* and *Viernes Santo*).
May 1: International Worker's Day (*Día del Trabajo*).
July 25: Saint James' Day (*Día de Santiago*).
August 15: Assumption (*Asunción*).
October 12: Spanish National Holiday (*Día de la Hispanidad*).
December 8: Immaculate Conception (*Concepción*).
December 25 & 26: Christmas (*Navidad*).
December 31: Balearic Day (*La Día de las Balears*).

Internet

Useful information and a calendar of events can be found on the Internet at www.mallorcaonline.com. Less lively, but offering just as much information is www.mallorca-topline.com. At the virtual travel agency www.toptravel.com, you can make hotel and finca reservations, as well as other transactions. If you cannot bear the thought of visiting Mallorca without being able to get on-line, try the Internet café *L@Red* (C. Concepció 5, Palma, tel: 971 713 574; Mon-Fri 3 pm-1 am, Sat and Sun 4 pm-1 am. For a virtual visit to this café, surf over to: www.laredcafe.com).

Language

Since the death of Franco, *Mallorqui*, a Catalan dialect, has experienced a renaissance. This is noticeable, for example, in the increasing use of the Catalan place names. This book uses only the "new" place names, even though the Spanish versions are still frequently used on the island. In the everyday language there are considerable differences from Castilian. But if you speak Spanish you will generally not have any difficulty. Besides, in many of the tourist resorts, English and German are the main languages.

Medical Care

In the Spanish *centres meicos* the personnel speak English. Since there are many British visitors and permanent residents on Mallorca, there are many English-speaking doctors and dentists with medical or dental practices on the island.

It is always advisable to take out some international/traveler's medical insurance before your visit. Most of the hospitals where English is spoken are found in Palma, e.g., Policlinica Miramar, Co. Vecinal de la Vilate s/n, 07011 Palma, tel: 971 455 212; Clínica Juaneda, C. Son Espanyolet, 55 Company 20, 07014 Palma, tel: 971 731 647. Other addresses that may be useful: The British Medical and Dental Centre, Paseo del Mar 30, Palma Nova, tel: 971 683 511 (24 hours); Portals Dental Practice, Plaça Alcázar 3, L6, Portals Nous, tel: 971 677 258, mobile phone: 989 578 121; Portals Medical Practice, Magna Plaça, Portals Nous, tel: 971 676 334 or 971 681 518 (emergency).

Nudism

Nude sun tanning and swimming are officially forbidden on Mallorca. They are, however, tolerated by the authorities on some sections of beach, e.g., at Es Trenc, near Colònia de Sant Jordi, in the southeast of the island, or at Cala Torta, in the northeast, near Artà.

Newspapers

English-language newspapers such as *USA Today* and the *International Herald Tribune* are available on Mallorca. All major English daily and weekly papers are also available, on their date of appearance, as are most major German, French, Dutch and Scandinavian newspapers. A weekly magazine for visitors, *Mallorca Magazine*, printed in English and German, is also available. Hotel receptions usually have copies.

Opening Hours

As in all Mediterranean countries, opening times are fluid and determined by the climatic conditions. Stores generally open between 9 and 10 am, and close for lunch at 1 or 1:30 pm. The siesta can last until 4 or 5 pm, after which stores stay open until 7 pm, many of them until 10 pm. Large supermarkets stay open all day. All stores are open on Saturday. On Sundays and holidays, small shops can usually meet basic requirements.

Banks are open Monday through Friday, from 8:30 or 9 am until 2 pm. On Saturdays they close at noon. The offices of various government authorities are usually open for public business Monday-Friday, from 9 am-1 pm, and 3-5 pm. Post offices are open Monday-Saturday, from 9 am-1 pm.

Pharmacies

A pharmacy is a *farmacia* in Spanish, and can easily be identified by a green cross on a white background. In addition to the regular opening hours there is a 24-hour emergency service listed at the door.

In general, all of the usual medical products are available on Mallorca. If you require special medication, however, be sure to bring an adequate supply for the duration of your visit; if you are flying, bring it in your carry-on baggage.

Post Offices

Post offices are called *correus* and, with the exception of the General Post Office in Palma (C. de la Constitució 5, tel: 971 721 867, Mon-Fri 8:30 am-8:30 pm, Sat 9:30 am-2 pm), are only open in the morning. In small towns in the interior, a postal van comes twice a week and serves as a post office. Letters and postcards remaining within Europe cost 70 ptas, outside Europe 80 ptas. If you wish to receive mail by poste restante, advise the sender to write *Llista de correus* on the envelope. You can buy stamps (*sellos*) in *estanc*, tobacco shops, and at newspaper stands in the main tourist centers.

Rural Tourism

The concept refers to a "gentle" kind of tourism that is generally practiced in the fincas (country houses) because it attempts not to overburden the environment. To qualify for this label, a rural tourism farmhouse must have been built before 1960, have a minimum area, and the owner must earn the major part of his income from agriculture. Brochures, information and reservations are available at: Associació Agroturisme Balear, 07006 Palma de Mallorca, Avda. Gabriel Alomar i Villalonga 8A, tel: 971 721 508, fax: 971 717 317. Or contact them by e-mail at: agroturismo@mallorcanet.com.

Telephones

The telephone code for Spain is +(34). Even when making local calls in Mallorca, you must use the area code for Mallorca, which is 971. If you wish to phone Mallorca from within Europe dial 0034 971 and the number you are calling; from outside Europe use your international dialing code plus 34 971. The number for mobile phones is +(34) 908.

For calls from Mallorca to the UK the code is 0044, followed by the local area code without the zero then the desired number. For calls to the USA and Canada use 001 before the area code.

You can use mobile phones for calls to, from and on Mallorca. The European GSM standard is available and the connections are good. In some valleys in the Tramuntana Mountains a few remote areas don't yet get reception.

The telephone number for general information is 1003; for international enquiries it is 1020.

Television and Radio

Better hotels have satellite dishes that receive international channels. English television channels are usually already programmed. English radio broadcasts can be heard on the BBC World Service, which operates in association with FM 98.5 Sunshine Capital Radio, Palma's local transmitter.

Time

In Mallorca, as in Spain, Central European Time (CET) applies, as does European Summer Time.

Mallorca is one hour ahead of GMT – 9:00 am in London is 10:00 am in Palma; six hours ahead of Eastern Standard Time (US/Canada east coast) – 9:00 am in New York is 3:00 pm in Palma; and nine hours ahead of Pacific Time (US/Canada west coast) – 9:00 am in Los Angeles is 6:00 pm in Palma.

Tipping

If you were satisfied with the quality of service, it is generally expected that you will keep to the internationally accepted practice of adding 10 percent to the total of the bill. In restaurants, bars, and cafés you receive the bill on a small plate. Place your payment on the same plate, upon which you will also receive your change.

Before you leave, place your tip on the same plate. If you are eating meals in your hotel, you should give the waiter a generous tip at the beginning of your stay; this should have a favorable influence on the service you receive during the rest of your stay.

Youth Hostels

Mallorca only has two youth hostels and they are often full during the peak season, so reservations are essential.

Alberg de Juventud, S'Arenal, C. Costa Brava 13, tel: 971 260 892. Reservations tel: 902 111 188.

Alberg de Juventud, Ca. Cabo Pinar at km 4 (La Victoria Peninsula, near Alcúdia), tel/fax: 971 545 395.

AUTHOR

Sebastian Melmoth studied German and Romance languages. He has been a lover of Mallorca for many years and on his numerous visits prefers to explore this charming Balearic Island by bicycle or on foot.

PHOTOGRAPHERS

Archiv für Kunst und Geschichte, Berlin 8, 22
Hackenberg, Rainer   3, 12, 19, 21, 39, 43, 53, 62, 68, 69, 70, 76, 78, 82, backcover top
Kolberg, Melitta   10/11, 63
Kut, Richard   40, 86
Möller, Gerd   85
Nowak, Gerald   16, 72
Pansegrau, Erhard   26, 55, 56, 60
Rein, Udo   17
Schraml, Oskar (Archiv G. Amberg)   35, 67
Schug, Bruno (Silvestris)   20
Semsek, Hans-Günter   79
Stankiewicz, Thomas   cover, 17, 32, 48, 52
Storck, Manfred   9
Stuffler, Jeanette   34, 46.